TRASH!

SIMON PARÉ-POUPART

TRASH!

A GARBAGEMAN'S STORY

TRANSLATED FROM THE FRENCH BY
PABLO STRAUSS

MELVILLE HOUSE
BROOKLYN • LONDON

Trash! A Garbageman's Story
First published in 2026 by Melville House

The translation of this work was made possible thanks to the financial support of the Société de développement des entreprises culturelles du Québec (SODEC)

First Melville House Printing: March 2026

Distributed by Penguin Random House LLC, 1745
Broadway, New York, NY 10019 USA.
www.penguinrandomhouse.com

Melville House Publishing
46 John Street
Brooklyn, NY 11201
and
Melville House UK
Suite 2000
16/18 Woodford Road
London E7 0HA

mhpbooks.com
@melvillehouse

ISBN: 978-1-68589-249-4
ISBN: 978-1-68589-250-0 (eBook)

Library of Congress Control Number: 2025951332

Designed by Beste M. Doğan

Printed in the United States of America
10 9 8 7 6 5 4 3 2

A catalog record for this book is available from the Library of Congress

The authorized representative in the EU for product safety and compliance is Easy Access System Europe, Mustamäe tee 50, 10621 Tallinn, Estonia.
gpsr.requests@easproject.com

Our relationship with garbage is an ambivalent one marked by attraction and repulsion. For the wealthy, garbage is anathema: dirty, inconvenient, a cause for concern. But the disadvantaged of the earth, and those excluded from productive labor—the unemployed, the disabled, retirees, prisoners, mentally ill people, and artists on the fringes—develop a firsthand acquaintance with what we throw away.

—CATHERINE DE SILGUY,
Histoire des hommes et de leurs ordures

CONTENTS

TRASH!

A LIFE IN GARBAGE

My experience of life is one that few will ever know. I spend my days surrounded by garbage. In twenty years, I've hauled nearly seventy thousand tons of trash, and this fact cannot help but shape the man I am today. The looks I get along my route show me that people sometimes mistake me for the trash I handle. But the way I see it, my job is of great consequence. I'm a garbageman. Day after day, I heave and haul the detritus of the most polluting civilization in human history. My fellow garbagemen and I scrub clean the stains of our consumer society. Our work behind the scenes keeps the whole edifice from crumbling down, at least for now.

I want to give you a glimpse of the world of trash as it came to be revealed to me: through a series of surprises. A happy coincidence, as it turns out, since I love my work. I'm telling my story because I want others to understand this passion of mine. I want the garbagemen of the world to be seen for what we are. Above all, I want you to stop believing that your waste disappears "by magic." Don't fall for the promise you've probably seen in ads for private haulers like 1-800-GOT-JUNK. Nothing disappears by magic. Let's leave these illusions for children and get back to the real world. It's a beautiful and dirty place—not unlike us garbagemen.

PART I

BECOMING A GARBAGEMAN

BAPTISM BY SWEARING: JESUS FUCKING CHRIST!

I'd promised myself I'd stop swearing. I have friends who are religious, and observant too, and I'd learned to refrain from offending them. I respect religion, though I'm not a believer myself. But when you jump off the garbage truck, squeeze between two badly parked cars, and come upon eighteen fifty-pound bags of construction waste . . . when you know this means you'll have to snake your way back through the cars without scratching them, holding the bags with your arms outstretched in front of you, all because the dickhead who filled them left the nails in the boards . . . when you're feeling the weight of the twenty tons of trash you've already lifted that day, and the bags are liable to burst open any second . . . and you know that if you get hurt in the process, that'll be on you, because you just weren't careful enough . . . and that if something gets damaged, that's on you too, and you're the one who'll have to clean up the mess, because no matter what happens, when you work for a big waste management company no one ever has your back . . . and you know perfectly well you shouldn't be picking up this guy's goddamned garbage, since he's flagrantly over the weight limit for roadside pickup . . . and he should just have done his job and taken it to the dump . . . and then, when you are almost out of breath, you look up and see the guy watching you through the curtains, with a look in his eye that makes it clear he'll be making a complaint if you don't pick up his bags—it's then, at that very moment, that the urge overcomes you and you let out a cry of rage: "*Jesus fucking Christ!!!*"

I mean, swearing is all you've got left. It may

offend God, but there's no better way to get your mind off that man's condescending look. The lack of consideration is what hurts most. He gets to hide behind his flowered curtains, this coward who can't even be bothered to properly dispose of his own construction waste. Smug fuckwits of his ilk are truly the worst. Knowing that he's the one who failed to take responsibility and seeing the sneaky way he's gone about it doesn't prevent me from feeling like a cleaner fish unceremoniously dumped into an aquarium. I'm the piddly creature that keeps the tank glass clean so the good middle-class people in their little boxes can admire their exotic fish through immaculate surfaces.

The garbageman came, the yard is clean, the grass will stay green. Now good riddance! That's what this guy's thinking as he closes his curtains. I may have made it through without a nail piercing my glove, but there's no time to celebrate. Sixty-five feet up the street, another pile of garbage is waiting at the roadside. This time it's neatly bagged. A little farther on, some crazy dude comes running after me with his bags. And then another calls out to get my attention. He's driven a mile with his garbage in the back of his car, petrified at the thought of it spending a week at his house.

The garbageman is the Sisyphus of our consumer society, a hapless laborer condemned to go from house to house picking up bags, swept along day after day in the never-ending flow of refuse we produce. And every day he is fated to resume this labor afresh, again and again, for all eternity. If we weren't there to shoulder this burden, everything would fall apart. The rats would take over, the air would turn fetid, plague and cholera would run rampant. George Bataille was right: excess is the accursed share of abundance, and no one can afford to get stuck with it.

That's one thing you learn in this business. The garbageman's yoke is destruction—the opposite of construction, the breaking down of things—and its wages are paid in the sweat on your brow and the pain in your flesh. Garbage juice may be the holy water of your baptism. But it's the swearing that makes you a real garbageman. That's when you truly become one with your function. You understand that you're nothing in the eyes of others, that you've got nothing to prove to anyone. You're at the bottom rung of society's ladder—but there's something reassuring in that, because you can't fall any lower. You're the living vestige of a bygone era, here in Quebec, at least: the age of the "working man." But not for you the patina of "working-class heroes" celebrated in popular culture, from Quebec's novels of rural life[1] to Zola's miners. Nobody writes novels about garbagemen. That doesn't leave us much to grasp onto, save the freedom that comes with a life on the margins and, in my case, the pleasure of physical labor.

Some take pride in this apostate status. It gives them a feeling of omnipotence. You know, *there aren't many people who could do my job*; *only real men can hack it*; *if they step on my truck I'll kick their asses*. Beneath the surface of this pride you'll find deep wounds, latent frustration, and even fragility. We are former bikers, dopers, athletes who've abandoned all hope of making the big time, grown-up kids scarred by tough childhoods. Violence is in our blood, and once we're thrown out into the world of waste disposal, it doesn't take long to rise to the surface.

Being a garbageman is itself an act of self-violence. The pace and physical demands of the work would not have been out of place in the first and second industrial revolutions. Some people think they'll find relief from their inner demons in the miracle of modern drugs. But drugs wear you out.

I've heard it said that the average garbageman lasts less than ten years behind the truck. Throwing trash takes a real toll. The human body only rarely achieves a level of stamina comparable to the machines we create. "He's a machine" is a compliment reserved for the very best garbagemen, and rightly so, because these men are as strong as the trucks they ride in. But when we outpace a machine, do we not lose something of our humanity? And isn't the fact that we're forced to work at this inhuman pace a sure sign that we're drowning in waste? Our assembly lines must keep spitting out new things for us to consume at an alarming rate, to keep the factories running and the cargo ships sailing and the airplanes flying and the pistons firing and the servers humming and the screens refreshing and the ads and notifications popping up day and night to goad us into desiring ever more. Our civilization manufactures new things at breakneck speed, only to have them fail ever more quickly. This keeps the wheels of commerce spinning. The end goal of this system is the obsolescence of all goods and all people—an acquiescent, clean, and happy obsolescence.

Sometimes it strikes me that there's a fundamental truth in the scene I described earlier. A decent-enough guy spying on me through his window to make sure his yard and house stay clean because he doesn't want to see that the real face of his world is us, the garbagemen.

BE A MAN!

I felt lost in my teenage years. Who doesn't, I know. But my case was complex. My parents' marriage had collapsed under the strain of my father's alcoholism. Nothing I could do had ever been good enough for him. And being worthless in my father's eyes had drawn me closer to my highly protective mother. Did she feel responsible for raising me with a dysfunctional father? Or was she just worried about my vulnerability? Either way, I was what you'd call a "mama's boy." I played Dungeons & Dragons, and I loved reading, and

I was certain that I'd be an intellectual one day. In my circle, that projected an image of weakness.

I later realized how common it is for garbagemen to grow up with an alcoholic or drug-addicted father. Intellectual aspirations? Not so much. I don't think I've ever met another who shared my dreams. In high school, I thought all parents expected their children to go on to higher education. But liking school didn't command respect where I grew up. No one in my house wanted to hear about Émile Zola over dinner, let alone Balzac. Getting an education was all well and good—if it led to a well-paid job. But this wasn't France. Learning for its own sake was nothing to take pride in. In Quebec, personal identity is defined not by cultural affiliations but by what a person does for a living.

My stepfather never tired of telling me to "*Be a man!*" His world was the gym, with its protein shakes and tanned, muscular bodies, everyone wanting to be Arnold Schwarzenegger; mine was school, polite behavior, and role-playing games. The writing was on the wall: the new man of the house wanted me to man up. My first reaction was derision. Laughing about the situation brought me some protection, and making light of my stepfather's version of who I was became my defense mechanism. I'd prance around the house imitating my stereotyped conception of a gay man, based on a character named Jean-Lou on the hit TV show *La petite vie*. Of course, this image of queerness was far too effeminate to be real. But before long I brushed up against the limits of self-mockery. Instead of confirming my identity, my vamping sowed seeds of doubt. I even began to wonder if there might be a modicum of truth in my stepfather's stupid jokes. And his macho persona was manifestly more attractive to girls than my effete tastes and mama's boy attitude. As this sank in, my adolescent self was shaken to the core.

"Jesus, Simon, make a man of yourself!" Hearing this insult so often made me feel the need to prove myself to others. I was obsessed with a song whose lyrics asked if anyone in the world had ever seen an intellectual with muscles.[2] *Make a man of yourself, make a man of yourself*, I thought. Well, why not? So I challenged my stepfather to help me get built. "Pierrot, what could I do to be a man?"

"Try doing a run behind a garbage truck," he answered. "That's supposed to be a tough job!"

He couldn't have given me a better suggestion.

AT THAT TIME, THERE WERE two ways to get into the garbage business. Either you knew someone who could hook you up—which, as you may have gathered by now, I did not—or you walked over to a truck and asked the guys how to get on with them. My stepfather was thrilled that I was at last heeding his advice. He called out to some guys on the side of the road and asked them for an address. Ever the model student but now determined to try my luck as a garbage collector, I went to drop off my résumé in person, as it was done in those days, at the headquarters on Montée du Domaine, a back road on the outskirts of the Montreal suburb of Saint-Eustache.

The company, Services Sanitaires Gauthier, was a small Quebec waste management outfit of the kind you saw before multinationals cornered the market. When I got there, I almost turned around on the spot. Looking out over the yard, I felt a million miles from my mother's comforting presence, my D&D games, and the university I planned to attend one day. Suddenly, I felt shaky. I was entering a strange new world, the world of garbage. Everywhere I looked, gutted trucks lay gaping like beached whales, their rotting carcasses drawing the scavengers circling overhead. A man with skin blackened by the grease he was applying to the trucks was going back and forth to the garage beside the office. Clouds of flies swarmed over heaps of garbage. Everything felt somehow outside of time, in a state of normality completely foreign to me. Yet this world I was experiencing up close for the first time was nothing new. I'd caught glimpses of it every time I walked by a garbage truck in the street or carried the garbage can in from the curb when I got back from school.

I wondered whether my unease was some sort of premonition. I felt out of my element. But I went into the office anyway and handed my résumé to a big guy. He was almost as filthy as the mechanic. A driver. He didn't even get up to greet me. He seemed as indifferent to my presence there as he was to my application. I wasn't sure where to stand, what to say . . . The situation was made all the more surreal by the fact that, ever the good student, I'd shown up with a neatly typed résumé printed on fancy paper and carefully placed in a folder. It detailed my schooling, my experience as a supermarket butcher's helper, my hobbies. I stood up straight, dressed in my interview clothes, and gave the man's hand a firm shake, even though I felt weak in the knees. In return, he barely deigned to look at me! He tossed my résumé aside with scarcely a glance and gruffly said he'd call me soon. And that was that. Not another word.

Daniel, the driver in question, had married into the Gauthier family, who were fairly big players in the Greater Montreal waste management business at the time. That was before Canadian, American, and later European multinationals moved in and pushed them out. But that's another story.

Daniel was in charge of hiring. Don't imagine exhaustive interviews or lengthy discussions. When you're hiring a garbageman, there's no need to waste a second longer than he spent on me, since the real test comes when you put the new guy on a truck. Why waste time in protracted discussions? Once you're out on the route, it's easy to see who can hack it and who can't. I'm confident that less than ten percent of people who try their luck on a garbage truck are going to work out. That's a lot of churn.

When I got my start in the business, the hiring process reflected the job's lawlessness. A lot of new people had an in, a brother or father or friend willing to convince the guys to give them a try. Often, a first shift would be worked for free, or in exchange for a few beers. Or your first day might be paid under the table, so if you didn't make the cut you could be let go with no hassle and no paperwork, just a "better luck next time."

Some new hires are so exhausted by the end of their first day that they forget to ask for payment. All they can think about is laying down their head to sleep. Afterward, they're too embarrassed to ask for their pay and you never see them again. In our business, managers live by the law of the jungle: Survivors live to work another day; everyone else disappears.

A WEEK AFTER I DROPPED off my résumé, I was woken up at dawn by my mom telling me to hurry off to Mirabel. I'd been called in by the company, Gauthier! I'd later learn that this is how it usually goes in the business. The companies are constantly short-staffed, and always on the lookout for new workers. They'll call you in the morning, the day before if you're lucky. In the best case, you'll know your schedule for the week; more often it's a day or two ahead of time. In my case, it was more like an hour or two.

It's summer 2003, and I'm in the Saint-Janvier neighborhood of Mirabel for my first shift as a garbageman. I'm waiting for the garbage truck to pick me up at a convenience store. I get out of my car and climb into the truck. Even this early in the morning it's hot, in the high eighties. A weather warning is advising people not to go outside, and to avoid strenuous physical exertion if they do. I'm working alongside Yannick, a onetime farmer who's now a helper—that's what we call the guys who run behind the truck picking up the garbage.[3] Yannick's wearing a tight tank top that shows off his bulging muscles, and he's quick, like an elf. He makes short work of emptying two garbage cans, one in each hand, into the top of the truck's hopper. I'm flabbergasted. Everything's moving so fast!

After working for a while, our route is interrupted when a small pickup pulls over, its reinforced bed laden with garbage. It had been cruising around the backroads of Mirabel, part of the route where the big ten-wheelers can't easily go. That's something you see in less densely populated areas: certain sectors are harder to collect—in winter, for example—or don't have enough volume to make it worthwhile sending out the full-sized truck. So lighter vehicles do the job.

The little pickup backs up until its bed is flush with the back of our garbage truck. Since I'm the new guy, I'm given a shovel and told to get into the box full of garbage.

"Hey, man. Load us up!" says Jean-Claude with a laugh, shooting the others a knowing look. I jump up into the bed, wading through layers of soft, smelly garbage. I climb on top of a pile of trash, striving to maintain my precarious balance while little white worms wriggle up my legs. I grab bags that burst open before I can manage to throw them into the hopper. The sun is beating down. I'm sweating, sinking into the mounds of garbage. It reeks. I'm starting to lose my bearings. I miss my bed, wonder what I'm doing in the middle of this heap of filth! I'm eighteen years old, starting junior college, reading Zola; I'm supposed to be preparing for a career, not wading through putrid piles of trash.

Little do I know that this new job will put me through college and ten years of university, alternating shifts behind a truck and days spent in the classroom and the library. Or that after earning first a bachelor's and then a master's degree, I'll keep right on throwing trash, where the physical challenge, camaraderie, and steady income balance out the intellectual satisfactions of other jobs in journalism, research, and social services.

But this eighteen-year-old kid has no thought for the future. He has his hands full struggling to empty the garbage from the bed of the pickup, and he eventually succeeds. The day goes on much in the same fashion, on and on and on and on for what feels like forever.

12:37 a.m. It's fifteen hours later and I'm still in Mirabel, still working the same shift! It's dark now, and slightly cooler than the daytime. I'm leaning up against the truck with my feet on the running board, barely able to keep my grip. I can see my elfin partner still going strong behind the truck, a flickering shadow darting to and fro in the darkness. His movements are quick, as vigorous as they were in the morning! I'm nodding off, exhausted.

Is this torture ever going to end?

I'm not sure how I got there, but at some point I realize I'm finally sitting in the cab. The day is done. The driver, peering at me from behind his glasses, tells me that my mother is waiting for me; she's been calling for hours. She wants to know what's going on with her teenage son. As I'm heading off, the driver shouts at me: "Hey kid, we'll pick you up tomorrow. Seven a.m."

Huh?

When I get home, I'm both exhausted and troubled. I feel confused, physically destroyed, but excited—as if I've experienced something monumental. It's hard to believe, but I can't wait to wake up and rejoin the crew whose life I now share. What these guys get done in a day boggles my mind. And I don't want to leave them shorthanded to face the work waiting for them. But still, I'm anxious. I have to get some shut-eye if I'm going to make it through another day like the one that just ended. I don't even have five hours to sleep! I'm spent. I didn't think it was humanly possible to demand so much from a human body.

I fall into a comatose sleep. But even then, my day comes back to haunt me. There I am, on the truck! The compactor blade is crushing and grinding me, and I'm caught in the hopper! Darkness closes in, I try to find the door . . . Is there even a door? There's no way to tell. I'm suffocating . . . I'm screaming for help! My mother and stepfather rush downstairs and wake me up. Less than three hours till I have to get up again. Fucking hell! I'm going to have to learn to sleep like a baby if I want to make a man of myself!

NIGHTTIME

Garbagemen love nighttime. A little too much, even.

Darkness and all that goes with it makes for perfect conditions for picking up trash—an activity you'd rather not see, carried out by people you'd prefer to ignore, whose purpose is to make the countless things you no longer want to see disappear. When night falls, we garbage collectors can fade into the background and embrace the weirdness of our lot. At nighttime, anything is possible. Trash cans thrown right into the compactor, unemptied; black bags left on the sidewalk—we didn't see them, or maybe didn't want to—yells and shouts that shatter the peace and quiet of sleepers. Darkness brings out the very worst in garbagemen. Trucks weave through traffic without a care, honking their horns and even sideswiping other vehicles without bothering to stop. And night is also when fights break out more readily. The nighttime streets belong to us.

Frank, who we call "The Runner," told me about a time some journalists showed up at the meeting spot of the Green World (GW) night crew. Green World had won contracts for a bunch of evening routes, before they got blacklisted and had to shut down. They were known for hiring the dregs of the industry, the very worst garbagemen active in those days. So at the meeting point, people were smoking, sniffing, and otherwise using as they got ready to start their shift. These were the guys who washed up at GW because no other company would have them. Guys like Jo, who got filmed by a Boucherville resident dancing on green bins in the midst of an intense mushroom trip. Racette, whose life cycled between garbage collection, rehab, and stints of homelessness; Cat, who would regularly get picked up by cops in the middle of his run; Brodeur, who threw compost bins in with the recycling . . . because they're made of plastic, after all. And Séguin, who'd get dropped off at the same corner where they had picked him up, since that's where he slept. Guys missing teeth, guys with tattoos, guys whose clothes looked like they came out of the garbage (and often did). Throw a bunch of guys like this together and you get a crew worse than the sum of its parts.

At the sight of this company of renegades, the journalists turned tail and left. The way Frank the Runner saw it, they were interested in telling the story of garbagemen, to a point—but not badly enough to spend an entire night with such a motley crew of human renegades. Frank would know; he was one of them. Today, he talks about these guys with a critical distance and an ironic perspective. But he never judges them. A former addict himself, Frank even went so far as selling his body for drugs. So he gets where these guys are at. When he was still using,

Frank was a hard case. I haven't forgotten how he constantly insulted me and put me down when I was starting out. He wasn't a "nice guy," by any stretch. When I remind him of those days, Frank apologizes, and also admits that there are entire stretches of his life he can't remember. He was just too wasted. As far as I'm concerned, Frank remains a force of nature. The guy can just keep running forever. He's as strong as his father, who was a garbageman too. Frank can actually ride a garbage truck like a human flag, with one hand on the running board and the other on a side bar, his body held sideways, *perpendicular to the hopper.* Trust me, it's sick.

Nighttime is when construction trucks roam the streets to illegally dump their waste under cover of darkness. That means our routes are littered with big bags full of glass and sharp nails. They're so heavy you have to prop them against your legs to lift them. It's a public menace. You don't know when you've cut yourself until you feel the warm blood running down your leg.

But night is also when the restaurant and bar patios in Montreal's Plateau district fill up. Well-lubricated patrons discover your existence and applaud your exploits, surprised to find themselves admiring a garbageman at work. Nighttime is when you recognize a well-known actress, shrieking in delight at the sight of you heaving a garbage can fifteen feet through the air to your partner, who catches it cleanly and slams it against the truck's inside wall, emptying it in one swift, perfectly executed motion. For a moment, in this place, at this unlikely hour, an audience forms that can appreciate the aesthetics of the work they look down on the rest of the time. You're seen running through a crowd of festivalgoers caught off guard by the sight of a bearded garbageman carrying twelve bags of trash, nimbly weaving between a young woman and her companion for the night.

When I started out, I wasn't part of the show that is Montreal nightlife. I worked on the city's fringes, where the suburbs seep into the countryside, and I'd often end up there very late at night. These days, that can't happen: only city workers do night routes, and private contractors get fined if their crews are out past a certain time of day. I'd ride behind the truck through the backroads of Mirabel, at speeds that only my inexperience would let me accept. We'd speed along from garbage can to garbage can, sometimes miles apart, as I held tight to the back of the truck. In front of me was the infinite darkness of the countryside; beside me, the huge hopper full of trash; all around me, dust mixed with the acrid smell of overheated tires and brake pads. Sometimes, the coolness of the fresh dew relieved my body of the heat it had spent all day building up. Not that you ever stopped for a moment to take in this scene, which had something poetic about it. All you knew was that you had to keep going, whatever the cost.

With my exhausted body, my repetitive movements, and my deep fatigue enshrouded in this night, I felt as if I'd already entered a dreamland long before I actually fell asleep. One driver once told me that sometimes, on his way home after an interminable night shift, he'd find himself stopping his Tercel in front of piles of garbage on the roadside, and then sit there waiting for some phantom worker to start loading the trash into his car.

I got it now. When my work was done and I'd finally gone to bed, my day would continue spooling out in my dreams, as if my body no longer knew how to rest. I'd sleepwalk. I'd wander around my room tossing things, as if I were still on a garbage truck. My poor mom couldn't figure out what was happening.

KIDS LOVE TRUCKS

I am concentrating so hard I don't notice her looking at me, or that she has a kid with her.

I should mention that, in Montreal's densely populated Plateau district, we collected the garbage at night in those days. Between the vehicle traffic, the lights, the bikes, the noise of the truck, and the pace I had to maintain, I wasn't paying much attention to pedestrians. Only when the lady and her kid stand right in front of me do I realize that they want to talk to me. She's smiling at me, which is a good start: it won't be another person ignoring my existence, or some whiner getting ready to lecture me on how to do my job.

No, it's something else. I look over to the child who is staring at me, eyes filled with admiration. Then the mother speaks to me.

"You know, my son's dream is to be just like you, when he grows up."

My answer comes to me spontaneously, without a second thought. Maybe, since this woman seems nice enough, I want to reassure her? I don't know. Whatever the reason, it comes out the way it comes out.

"Don't worry. He'll get over it."

When kids see the garbageman, sometimes even *their* garbageman, they fall in love. He's their idol. They're so impressed by the truck that they worship the man who seems to tame its force, unafraid of its growling engine and its iron maw. Children are entranced by the garbagemen in the same way we have always admired heroic lumberjacks like Paul Bunyan in the United States or Jos Montferrand in Canada, strongmen from Heracles to Louis Cyr, the fearless log drivers that once plied our rivers . . . Kids just can't get enough of us. They're the only ones who can look beyond the dirt and the smell to love us.

How is it that this child who looks at me with admiration will grow into an adult who will at best fail to see me and at worst despise me? The answer is, of course, socialization: the transmission of values that slowly but surely draw a line between decency and dirt. When this little boy grows up, he'll cease to dream of garbagemen. He'll have understood that we belong in the realm of filth, a place better left unexplored.

Social reproduction is a powerful force. The sociologist Luc Boltanski, whose work has looked at the tendency of doctors' children to become doctors themselves, is a powerful example. Family and social backgrounds, not individual choices, make doctors. My own experience on the ground has taught me that alcoholic fathers are a common thread in the early lives of garbagemen. One thing is sure: I've never heard of a doctor's son running behind a truck, any more than I've ever seen a garbageman's son become a doctor. Garbagemen are born, and only rarely made. You could say it's a family business, passed on from father to son and from brother to cousin, as if whole fleets of family members find themselves lashed to the truck's running boards.

For certain social classes, the world is an immaculately clean and well-mannered place; for others, a destiny of dirt, toil, and low status awaits.

Take my buddy, "The Legend" (he's the one who insists on that moniker). When he dropped out of school, his father gave him a choice: "Kid, if you aren't going to school, you're coming out on my truck!" So he got his start in the trade at age sixteen. The hard way. The Legend was a little bully when he was a teenager, a cocky little bastard, and not an especially brilliant one. He's the type of guy who, had he been born to wealth, would be grinding his competitors to dust in the business world. He has that winning combination of smugness, cunning, and unscrupulousness required to rise to the top in business. But he comes from where he comes from, so he isn't going anywhere. His two sisters are dating garbagemen, and his father's a garbageman too.

It reminds me of the weird and wonderful Brodeur clan, from Pointe-Calumet near Montreal. The father was known as "Rock'n'Roll," a word used in Quebec French to suggest a wild ride with a whiff of danger. After a youth spent as a doorman in clubs, Rock'n'Roll was still driving a garbage truck at age seventy—with an IV drip in the cab. He had throat cancer, I think, and was administering his own treatment. Now there's a man who loved the game. He kept his crew flying. When I worked with him in Laval, I broke my tonnage records. And his two sons were just like him: proud, and plenty scrappy. The oldest one was constantly fighting during working hours. He was impossible to manage—but wow, what a machine! The younger one, a tall, lanky dude whose appearance belied incredible reserves of strength, moved so fast it looked like he was pushing the truck forward. He always worked alone. There was just no point adding a second man behind the truck, not to mention the danger a second helper would be in. Because the younger Brodeur tossed cans into the truck the way kids throw their toys during tantrums. Blindly, and fueled by rage. No one wants to take a twenty-five-pound trash bag in their face.

Another old-timer who was still on a truck past age seventy was Papy. This keen-eyed former farmer, patriarch of the Gratton clan, worked a route in Laval. Papy was cheerful. One of Papy's sons, whose name, Shoushoune, suggests a puppy-dog persona, was a helper. The other, Stéphane, drove trucks. Stéphane once told me that there was no way he would let his own kids run behind a truck. He wanted better for them. He wouldn't even let his son get a summer job collecting garbage, out of fear that the social environment would contaminate him. Stéphane had chosen to fight back against the powerful forces that tied his family to the working-class world. But these ties that bind are hard to break.

Socialization is the force that teaches us that collecting garbage is a shitty job, at least in others' eyes, and that becoming a garbageman makes you some sort of pariah. But socialization is also what teaches us to resist this characterization and reject the identity imposed on us by the outside world. We do this by choice, sometimes, and often simply out of pride. For the most part, garbagemen understand and accept their social status. Few have finished high school, but that doesn't mean they're stupid. They know they're not doctors. But deep down, they also know that under other circumstances, they could have been.

The garbageman lives on the margins of society. He's a nonconformist out of necessity. A rebel without a cause, chaotic, pathetic, fiercely independent, an inverted image of normal life. It might be this sense of flouting established order that so appeals to kids. In any event, as a person who has been to university and made the conscious choice to become a garbageman, because I wholeheartedly subscribe to these values, I can say that that's what I admire about these guys.

GARBAGE DOESN'T LIE (I)

DOWN AND OUT

Spandex lives in a shack down by the river, Rivière des Mille-Îles, to be precise. It's a bare-bones version of a house, slightly crooked and short a few teeth, not unlike the man himself. Though his real name is Michel, the guys call him Spandex for the shorts he likes to work in. Spandex runs behind a truck shirtless, in flip-flops and bike shorts, a surprising getup even for a garbageman. When he was thirty, Spandex robbed a convenience store with a sawed-off shotgun. Or at least tried to. The owner disarmed him and beat him up. As you can imagine, that dealt a serious blow to his street cred.

It's hard not to break out in a smile at the sight of Spandex out on his run, picking up the trash with his gut jiggling around, with nothing but flip-flops on his feet and his bike shorts on his ass. The young kids on the truck—guys just passing through the trade, for the most part—like to have a good laugh at his expense. Success of any kind always just seems to slip through Spandex's fingers.

And it's true no one knows much about Michel. Except for one thing: he talks to the trash. It's like he'd rather have a conversation with a garbage bag full of vegetable peels or broken bottles than human beings. He tells the garbage all about the weather and fills it in on what's new in his life. Now, Spandex isn't heartless: he also asks the garbage how *it's* doing, despite the cold, mud, and heat, and the worms eating away at what few shreds of dignity these once-proud castoffs are still clinging to. How did Spandex get into this unusual habit? No one really knows. Some say it's the outcome of a life stacking up failure after failure, a sense of shame, a response to the mockery of others. Of course, it could also just be good old-fashioned substance abuse.

I have a different theory, though. It comes from Victor Hugo's *Les Misérables*, where you'll find a lovely long passage about the sewers of Paris.

> The sewer is the conscience of the city. Everything there converges and confronts everything else. In that livid spot there are shades, but there are no longer any secrets. Each thing bears its true form, or, at least, its definitive form. The mass of filth has this in its favor, that it is not a liar.

I believe that Victor Hugo's observation is close to the reason Spandex carries on dialogues with the garbage: All is laid bare in the trash. Secrets and false appearances fall away, and everything at last shows its true face and definitive form. And I think this ultimate honesty we find in the trash must be soothing for Spandex.

Victor Hugo and Michel Spandex both grasped an essential truth that eludes all but a chosen few. They understood that our garbage speaks to us, and that its honesty can come as a relief. Once it reaches the end of its service life, the refuse produced by our society is stripped bare of all illusion. It reveals the sometimes-unsettling, unaccommodated face of all we cast off. Garbage bursts our mirages, puts everything on equal footing, and tells the whole story—if you know how to listen.

BREAKING THE RULES

TI-CHRIS

Spring 2004, in the Montreal suburb of Saint-Eustache. The crew from Gauthier's waste disposal is taking a break at a poutine stand. We're sitting around a picnic table, chatting and basking in the sun. A joint is going around, from helper to helper and then to the driver, who passes it back to the helper on his right. A normal, laid-back, everyday scene—until, out of nowhere, Ti-Chris leaps to his feet. (His nickname translates roughly as "little shit," a curse of endearment usually reserved for unruly kids). We watch him in surprise. Without a word, he sprints off from the table, hops a fence, and disappears into the fields, leaving behind his fries and his friends. He'd seen a cop, damn it! Best not to take any chances. So long: Ti-Chris was done for the day. His abrupt flight gave us all something to laugh about. And every time we bring it up, we have another good laugh.

He was back the next day, as if nothing had happened.

When I first met Ti-Chris, whose given name is actually Christian, he was strong as Samson, with a pretty-boy mug like Brad Pitt. A hard-working, dependable guy whose angelic face and childlike kindness must have tempted the devil. Whatever the reason, Ti-Chris fell prey to the worst temptations and some serious vices. He got into coke, bad. Perpetually short of cash, living in a sad apartment in western Laval and dancing the night away in gay bars, his life was a mess; he was wasted all the time. The man got to be so slack-jawed that when he tried to talk, you'd swear he'd been smacked with a crow bar. I mean, he was struggling to hold down his garbageman job, which is saying a lot. By the end, the mere sight of a policeman was enough to spook him.

Then, in 2010, when I imagine Ti-Chris must be dead or otherwise lost forever, he shows up behind my truck while I'm working in Laval-Ouest. Surprise, surprise, he jumps up on the running board.

"Well, well, Ti-Chris! Where've you been?" I ask.

He's no longer a garbageman, for obvious reasons, but when he saw me he decided to give me a hand. He just hopped on to finish the neighborhood with me.

Thing is, before he went off the rails, the guy was a phenomenon. Rock, his onetime driver, swears to me that he once saw Ti-Chris pick up a washing machine and throw it into the hopper, with one hand, *without stepping off the truck's running board*. The guy I ran into again years later may have been a shadow of his former self, but he was still a standup dude. And he still had some legs on him—enough to run with me for a while, but not enough to outrun his demons. I never saw Ti-Chris behind a truck again.

GARBAGE ADDICTS

Fall 2021. We're in the Ahuntsic neighborhood in northern Montreal, which appears to be gentrifying fast. I'm working for Ricova, a medium-sized recycling company with a strong presence in Montreal. It was formerly known as Green World, but the word is that they got so many complaints under that name they were forced to shut down. Ricova operates on a brokerage basis: its collection contracts are subcontracted to small-time local operators. The company's reputation may be better than GW's, but it has nonetheless managed to earn a spot on the City of Montreal's blacklist, for contract fraud. So maybe you never get a truly clean slate.

Ahuntsic is where I first meet a driver named Steve. Right away the chemistry is good between me, him, and the other helper, a young guy from a tough neighborhood called Hochelaga. This helper may be young, but he's been working in garbage collection since he was fourteen.

The three of us are really flying, set to finish early

if we keep up this pace. In between the garbage cans we're tossing back and forth—we do this to speed things up by cutting down the number of steps—the other helper tells us how he got stabbed in the middle of the street, on his way out of a bar. Over a woman. And how ever since it happened he's been keeping an eye out for the guy who did it. How he's going to "take him out."

Steve and I decide to take the truck to the dump to unload while the helper from Hochelaga stays out on the route, gathering up the remaining garbage cans to places our truck can actually stop, which will make our job a lot easier.

"We're killing it!" says Steve on the way to the dump. "You're really running, it's wild. Makes me want to put on my shoes and go out back with you!"

For some reason, I'm surprised to hear it from him.

"You used to run. Were you good?"

The driver turns to me, smiling.

"Man, I used to run just like you. I never quit. And before that, I was with the Hells [Angels]. I was unstoppable. I needed that rush, and I got it doing deliveries, for the bikers. Being a garbageman was my ticket out of there. I had all kinds of problems, and the solution was on the back of the truck. The same adrenaline rush I'd get trying to get away from the cops, with my coke . . . well, the only other place I found that is on the garbage truck. That's what let me stop doing deliveries. There was even a shrink, told me garbage saved my life!"

"That's a hell of a story."

"Oh, I'm not the only one. I was running with the Hells. Bidoux [another driver, who I also know] was with the Rock Machine. We traded one trip for another."

Of all the addictions I've seen, Steve's is my favorite. Maybe because I get it: I'm also addicted to the rush of running behind a garbage truck.

OLD ANDRÉ

Old André was one of the first helpers I ever worked with. When we met he was fifty-two, with graying hair slicked back and forever covered by a dirty, faded cap that sat crooked on his head. Picture your mental image of a paragon of fitness. Now imagine the opposite. That's André: smoke in his mouth, big stout gut, and always a beer on the go somewhere in the truck. There was nothing graceful about the man's style. Both carrying his body and carrying the garbage seemed to demand a painful effort from him. When he worked, his face would screw up into terrible grimaces.

And yet—the old guy just kept on going. He could run for ten hours, if that was what it took. Meeting Old André blew my mind. He was truly built different. I'd never seen anything like it. He was an athlete of a kind I'd never come across or known about: a real working man.

André was in most ways a typical garbageman of his generation: heavy drinking, but not into drugs. The younger ones, my generation, prefer smoking weed. Some take speed, to boost their performance, and others do harder drugs, for the high. But you don't find many alcoholics. And you definitely don't get many like me who lead relatively healthy lives. I work out, I try to eat a healthy diet, and when I get home, I don't spend the rest of the night getting bombed. I grew up with a mom who was there for me, who looked after me and taught me how to live well, and who protected me from my dysfunctional, violent, alcoholic father who could have destroyed my self-esteem. My upbringing made me keenly aware of my limitations. For all these reasons I have always worked in the garbage business, but only part-time. That way I can stay in shape, and pursue other projects, like writing a book.

You won't find many garbagemen who age well. I'm thirty-nine now, and for at least five years people have been asking me if I'm going to stop running soon.

BEAUJEUNEHOMME

It's early in the morning, and my day starts off on Avenue des Pins, in Montreal's Plateau district. As we're picking up the very first bins, Beaujeunehomme rolls up. The nickname, which means "handsome young man," is clearly a relic of the past. Beaujeunehomme isn't young anymore, and as for handsome, let's just say he's not what he used to be.

Though it's eight in the morning, he's drunk. Although drunk doesn't cover it. Beaujeunehomme is pissed to a degree that's hard to fathom. His face has that telltale red tint from high blood pressure, his eyes are yellow, and it's not hard to imagine that if you made an incision in his arm a stream of alcohol would spurt out. I let the driver know, and he tells the boss. The answer? Don't worry: it's just Beaujeunehomme's normal state.

So we carry on. Beaujeunehomme is fifty-two, and running around in a state of inebriation that would make even the hardest drinkers stagger. Yet I know plenty of people who could show up stone cold sober, and in perfect health, and not come close to working as hard or as well as he's managing to do. It's kind of sad that there's no award for this rare ability.

Despite his spectacular work ethic, Beaujeunehomme has hit a dead end in the industry. He doesn't have a driver's license, so he can't climb the only ladder within reach and start driving the truck. It may seem surprising, but making the move to driver is what finally helps many garbagemen outrun their problems.

It's not a cushy job by any means, and it comes with heavy responsibility. The driver is in charge of everything—the crew, the route, and of course the truck itself.

On the personal front, Beaujeunehomme is also in a rut. He's living on his own. His girlfriend has left him, and his daughter doesn't want to see him anymore. But he keeps right on trying to save money, for her sake. He talks about it with pride, gets emotional. She's at university. Beautiful, bright, and healthy, and Beaujeunehomme loves her. He's always waiting for her call, but isn't holding his breath.

Beaujeunehomme lives in a basement apartment in Laval, across the river from Montreal. His place is furnished with mismatched flea market furniture he's picked up here and there. Everything Beaujeunehomme owns is worn out. The man has a thousand and one great stories to tell—tales of inheritances, financial investments, and Ali Baba's caves, a trove of treasures he's owned and then lost.

Beaujeunehomme's tales of woe are like a slow-motion car crash. You can't look away. But there's something endearing about them. His buddies—all garbagemen themselves—love the guy. They all know Beaujeunehomme's life will come to an abrupt end one day—and I think they're good with that. Sure, his benders are the stuff of myth and legend, but the brokers always hire him back anyway. Everyone in the garbage business accepts him just the way he is, unconditionally, few questions asked. Sometimes keeping your mouth shut is an elegant way to love someone.

Beaujeunehomme is a castoff who feels right at home surrounded by garbage.

JO

Word has gotten around: a broker that I've worked for before is losing its contract in Montreal's Saint-Michel district. When that happens, the guys start jumping ship, before it sinks altogether. And if a broker is so short-staffed that they can no longer service a route, they can face hefty fines from the City. Add in the fees incurred by the subcontracting firm, and the broker can be staring down bankruptcy.

For the mercenaries of the garbage business—people like me—the misfortunes of brokers are great news. Since I don't work full-time, I'm not at the mercy of any one boss. I sell my services to the highest bidder. And when a broker finds itself short-staffed, I can choose to help them out—for the right price. The broker knows it's better off overpaying me than breaching its contract.

That's how I find myself here, at the meeting point in Saint-Michel. The man driving the truck is my old acquaintance, Frank the Runner. And once I'm in the back, I realize that the other guy I'm running with is Jo. Amazing. He's one of the first guys I worked with, back when I was just eighteen. A real athlete, who could be counted on to knock off the most demanding routes. *Intense* is a good word to describe Jo. He'd run behind the truck with his mouthpiece on, all day, to train his breathing for his boxing class later that evening. But the man I see opening the truck door looks less fit than the Jo I once knew. I watch him with concern, out of the corner of my eye. His movements are jerky, disjointed, more robot than human.

He contorts himself into strange positions, goes off on weird tangents. His mouth is pasty. I say hi. Jo can barely get a word out.

"He's having a bad trip," Frank explains.

It's 6:55 a.m.!

We assess the situation. Even Frank, who used to be a serious drug user, is in shock. We talk about Jo as if he weren't there, which in his current state isn't far from the truth. He looks like he might keel over and die right here in the truck. We're not sure what we should do: Take him to a hospital? Let him work anyway?

As we're talking, our fucked-up buddy somehow manages to open the cab door, put his feet up on the running board, and jump down onto the ground. When the first garbage cans come into view, he springs into action like an automaton. At first his movements are freakish and chaotic, but with time they grow more precise, until they achieve a surprising smoothness. I start working with him. We polish off the route in record time.

Etched deep in our brains is the trace of the moves we repeat day after day. Our bodies don't soon forget. Jo's, for one, remembers.

In any other job, an employee who shows up bombed out of their skull will be shown the door. But here's the thing: even as stoned as he was, *Jo still managed to keep up with me*. Whenever we got a break or he experienced a rare moment of lucidity, we'd catch up. It's the usual litany, same as it ever was: emotional crises, struggling to see his children, a strained relationship, living in an apartment with a bunch of other garbagemen, in debt up to his eyeballs.

Jo fills me in on one of the brokers that subcontracts for a larger firm, which has made loan-sharking an integral part of their operations. I imagine Jo must be in pretty deep with them. He explains that the broker pays bail when a garbageman ends up in jail. Then they hire the guy and garnish his wages to pay off the debt—with interest, of course. As business models go it may be twisted, but it's sadly not uncommon. I've known brokers that find out all about their employees' purchases, figure out how much they owe to their bank or in car loans. This information gives the brokers a sense of how much control they'll be able to exert. It's not uncommon for helpers to get into debt with their brokers, just as brokers often go bankrupt. You could even say that these two players in the garbage economy are bound together by chains of debt. One is indebted to the little boss, the other to the big conglomerates, which are themselves no doubt in debt to big banks. As the anthropologist David Graeber reminds us in his book *Debt: The First 5,000 Years*, capitalism is a chain of indebtedness that firmly ties individuals to wage labor and has never been organized primarily around labor freely consented to by workers. Even before we've lived our lives, we owe them to our employers and financial institutions.

It reminds me of a moving and fascinating book by Chris Hedges and Joe Sacco. *Days of Destruction, Days of Revolt* depicts poverty in the United States, and it reminds me in many ways of the garbage business. We read about how many Latinos, who are often not full-fledged U.S. citizens, work in the fields of Florida and other states, often completely under the yoke of big farmers. It's a sophisticated form of slavery. And it's the lack of freedom that is so abhorrent in this brutal form of capitalism.

In Quebec, you can make a decent living as a garbageman. But if the wages of your job include your freedom, and your work doesn't provide a degree of social mobility and independence from big business or sketchy brokers, then you're not really further along. The abject poverty that brought you to the garbage business in the first place will only keep getting worse and worse. I imagine that's how it went for my pal Jo.

POMPON

Most mercenaries in the garbage business have certain things in common. They tend to take a degree of enjoyment in being close to waste. They understand that their socially and economically precarious working conditions encourage abuse and exploitation but still feel fairly comfortable operating within this world because they're not themselves tied down by debt. And since they know they can walk out the door any time, they don't give a damn about their bosses.

But power struggles and compromises can take surprising turns. Like what happened when Pompon, a former helper who's a driver now, got in a disagreement with his boss over those very working conditions. Their "negotiations" quickly soured, and a pissed-off Pompon grabbed a shovel to clock his boss in the head. He started chasing him around the property of the larger company that subcontracted to the broker. In the end, no shovel-blows were dished out. Pompon took off. And after a while he was rehired, *by the same broker*, on one condition: any truck Pompon was assigned to wasn't allowed to carry the usual shovel on the side. An occupational health-and-safety measure.

FACEBOOK

I'm clicking through Facebook posts from garbagemen looking for work. What's striking is how many of them demand, right out in the open, to be paid cash (i.e., under the table). Others mention they've completed therapy, or stopped drinking or using. In other fields, being fresh out of rehab isn't generally what you list on the top of your résumé! But garbagemen do things differently.

For one small broker I knew, hiring workers coming out of rehab or therapy was a point of pride. Another broker I knew also welcomed guys with addiction issues, and not because he wanted to take advantage of them. A lot of people might picture the garbage business as a retrograde world, but in fact, it's admirably open-minded. I worked with one driver who was only allowed to leave his live-in rehabilitation center for his shift driving his truck.

Stop and think about the meaning of *rehabilitation*. When your life goes sideways, what you need most to get back up on your feet is to not be judged. One thing the garbage community offers everyone working in it is the chance to keep on being who they are, making progress at their own pace, by holding down a job. Garbagemen are held in such low social esteem that no one really pays attention to their existence. And that contempt isn't all bad, from our point of view. Garbagemen live life free of the scrutiny of others, with all its attendant pressures. With no identity to lay claim to or defend, garbagemen can't climb the social hierarchy, because they're stuck forever on the bottom rung.

LOST LIVES

Every form of social order produces waste, a concept sociologist Zygmunt Bauman explores in his book *Wasted Lives: Modernity and Its Outcasts*.[4] There's always a boundary between clean and dirty, pure and impure. But a world like ours, shaped by an obsession with progress, has one particular feature: the more goods we accrue, and the greater the comfort we enjoy, and the cleaner our surroundings are kept, the more waste it produces, from the junk that fills our landfills to the "wasted" existences of fellow human beings. "The excluded are not the 'exploited' but the outcast, the 'leftovers,'" said Pope Francis.[5]

Our world generates a glut of both actual garbage and what Bauman terms "human waste." He notes that the globalized economy is crushed under the weight of this human waste, which cannot be recycled or swept up. In this category of people for whom society can't find a place, Bauman includes children in slums, and migrants undertaking perilous journeys or languishing in camps on the borders of rich countries.

It's the people condemned to living in filth, drug addicts, and the hordes of "unproductive" people, the ones who never had a chance—all of those who do not "add value" to the world economy, in the capitalist calculus. And this group of people is growing every day.

I understand that certain readers may be put off by some of the stories I've been telling, and by others that are coming up. This rogue's gallery of eccentric garbagemen, people living out hard lives after tough childhoods, deviants, and rejects, may give you pause. Am I exaggerating, for the sake of the story? Or, worse, are garbagemen a real public menace? Should we trust a guy pulling on a joint in the driver's seat of a ten-wheeler? Should we really be letting these criminals roam the streets of good neighborhoods?

All corporations today put a great deal of effort into "reputation management." They adopt "best practices," hire brand managers, get themselves nice websites and immaculate offices. "Deviant" employees are disciplined, or never hired in the first place, as companies grow less and less willing to hire weirdos. You might find these signs of "progress" reassuring.

Well, not me.

The world of garbage is a Wild West, and that's exactly what I love about it. I love straddling the fine line between dirty and clean. I love the joyful chaos of garbagemen, our anarchic spirit and vague desperation. I could justify this by telling you that if I were to choose between the squabbles and revenge fantasies of my coworkers and the lawyered-up criminality of transnational waste disposal corporations, I know where my sympathies lie . . . I could make arguments about the impunity of the rich and the hypocrisy of the middle classes . . . But the truth is more complex. I love the chaos of the garbage truck *for its own sake*. It gives me a space of freedom I can't find anywhere else. Offer me this deal and I'm all in, without equivocation or qualification. So when corporations and governments come along with plans to regulate and organize this chaos, it does nothing for me. Is it necessary? Maybe. But I'd prefer not to.

It seems eminently reasonable to me to maintain a gray area, one where those who struggle to find their place in society can form a community. Try to conceive of it as a recycling system for "human waste." Call it social ecology, or reintegration in society. You could think in terms of solidarity among outcasts, a miniature society of people unfit for mainstream consumption, a self-management scheme for deviance, a universal brotherhood of trash. I call it me and my garbageman buddies.

I ran into Ti-Chris again not long ago. An outcast among the outcasts, he has now been expelled from the brotherhood of garbagemen as well. He's collecting scrap metal. It's one of the few businesses where a guy like him can be recycled and get a fresh start. Even if some of the income may not find its way onto a tax return, giving a new life to objects cast off and left for dead is honest work. Some might see collecting scrap as a sign that you've fallen low. I see it as a sign of hope.

PART II

THROWING TRASH

GARBAGE DOESN'T LIE (II)

THROWAWAY

In 1955, *Life* magazine published a photo of a nuclear family tossing plastic and aluminum plates, cups, and utensils, which appear to rise up into the air like a flock of birds. The celebratory title is "Throwaway Living."

The Age of Waste was off to a gleeful start. Welcome to a brave new life of ease, where nothing has to be maintained, washed, cared for, or otherwise saved. Seventy years on, this dream of disposability has turned into a nightmare. The figures are staggering. Annual production of solid waste now tops 2 billion tons worldwide, and is expected to reach 3.8 billion tons by 2050.[6] There is nowhere left—not even outer space!—that is not strewn with human garbage. Nearly 10,000 tons of trash are currently orbiting Earth. Maybe I should send my résumé to NASA.

Until the late nineteenth century, the word *waste* meant something different than what it means in today's consumer society: any object left behind by its owner, for whatever reason. In the past, planned obsolescence on a massive scale was not something conceivable to the human race.

Credit for the term *planned obsolescence* normally goes to Bernard London, a Russian-born New York real estate broker who penned a series of papers on how this notion could end the Great Depression and serve as a foundation for a prosperous economy.[7] The first of these, "Ending the Depression through Planned Obsolescence," was written during a lull in real estate sales in 1932, the same year as Aldous

Huxley's *Brave New World*, in which many parallels can be found. London's enthusiastic argument for planned obsolescence of products and even buildings to drive economic growth now seems prescient, even if he believed government regulation, not markets themselves, would be the means to achieve this.

The modern English word *waste* has come down to us through Old French and, earlier, Latin *vastare* (to lay waste, to ravage) and *vastus* (empty, desolate). Waste was conceived as any excess not used in the manufacture or transformation of an object: things like fabric scraps, the modest scraps of a humble, thrifty world.

The French word for garbage is *ordure*, derived from the Latin *horridus*, meaning "horrible." It originally meant a kind of compost created by excrement, bones, and peelings, a sludge that was reused to fertilize the fields. For a long time, garbage was an integral part of the cycle of life. Today, it is seen as a threat to that way of life. This change has a name: progress.

"DON'T COMPLAIN, YOU CHOSE YOUR JOB!"

I'm in the Notre-Dame-de-Grâce, better known as NDG, a neighborhood on the west side of the island of Montreal. Many people think of NDG as an English-speaking neighborhood, although its lingua franca is that classic Montreal mix known as *franglais*. I'm working on a recycling truck—"on recycling," as we say. Goddamned recycling. I don't know who came up with Quebec's recycling system in its current form, but that guy has some answering to do. It's a poorly conceived mess.

For garbagemen of my generation, there's an undisputed hierarchy. Garbage collection is for real men, recycling is for amateurs, and compost is beneath contempt. Some people, including most of the old-timers, won't touch compost. And that's saying something.

Any guy who claims to actually like doing recycling and chooses it over garbage is considered suspect, likely a weakling who can't hack the real deal. Because the original garbageman's job—the foundation of our profession—is garbage collection. It stands to reason that if you want to call yourself a garbageman, you have to collect garbage.

My own theory is that this hierarchy is actually based on a criterion that few garbagemen would be able to articulate: our autonomy, the degree to which we are free to control what we actually do on the job. The more workers feel free to steer the course of their work, the less they feel supervised, the more they'll enjoy it. And on that front, when we're throwing trash, we're the freest of the free. Compost quickly degenerates into a bureaucratic shitshow.

That said—things are changing as the amount of pure garbage collection we do diminishes. In 2021, an average individual in Montreal discarded around one thousand pounds of waste (1020.74, to be precise), and this figure is expected to drop to under nine-hundred pounds (879.64) by 2025. Our landfills are overflowing, and the people in power want as little waste as possible to end up in them.

To spare our landfills, the share of recycling and composting in waste collection is on the rise, and so too, no doubt, is the status of the people who collect them. When you pick up garbage versus recycling or compost, you can fill up a truck in less time. Your loading time is faster. And your movements are more varied. As the day goes on, you can feel yourself getting a real workout. If there's enough tonnage along your route, it will rarely take more than four hours to fill up a load. Some trips take as little as two hours, or less. As a worker, it gives you a satisfying sense that you're getting shit done.

From an athletic standpoint, it's a complete workout, not unlike a CrossFit session. And as an added bonus, on some runs you get the chance to find stuff worth keeping for yourself or valuable scrap metal. There's money to be made there! It's even not unheard of to get tips—something that'll never happen on the compost route, and only very rarely on recycling. I guess the less environmentally friendly the activity, the more generous people are.

What about the compost run? For starters, it feels interminable. Bins are often tiny, so filling a truck can take five or six hours. That's a long time! To give you a sense of what it feels like, imagine how much less fun it would be to play a soccer game in which you were only allowed to walk—one foot had to be kept on the ground at all times—versus running full speed and jumping and dribbling the ball.

Factor in the lower tonnage of organic waste for an equivalent population density, and the result is that compost routes cover a much larger area. And at every stop you pick up the same tiny and unergonomic brown bins. More often than not, the container weighs more than its contents. But then, at other times, the compost is so heavy that you drag that brown thing over to the truck with your back folded over like a weeping willow bending under the weight of its leaves. I'm not saying that when you're on garbage duty you can *always* lift in an ergonomically correct fashion, but at least the bins, which are the work of industrial designers, show a higher degree of consideration for the garbagemen who will use them. And last but most definitely not least, working garbage you have a huge range of shapes and sizes of cans, bins, bags, and objects. You aren't performing the exact same movement over and over again.

With those fucking brown miniature bins, though, it's the *exact* same movement—a horrible movement—over and over again! To save time, you have to reach into the bin and transfer the contents to another bin. So far, not bad. The catch is that organic matter is teeming with life. It heats up, and sometimes the bags burst open halfway through the process, spilling their foul-smelling contents all around you . . . and on you. After that you can expect your hands to stink for days, even if you wash them like a maniac. Want to know what a city smelled like during the Middle Ages? Take a shower in compost bin juice.

Collecting recyclables falls somewhere in between garbage and compost. It's not overcontrolled, per se, just poorly organized. The bins and boxes have all clearly been designed, selected, and purchased by people who've never been on the back of a garbage truck. And of course, no one ever thought to ask our opinion! Do you think we're actually smart enough to have good ideas about the best design for the bins we work with? The result of not asking is that many of these bins are heavier than the recyclables themselves. It's hard on the back, as my chiropractor will tell you. It doesn't help that residents rarely put them out facing the right way, and municipalities don't bother pressing the point. Specifically, I'm talking about the massive 240-liter recycling bins on wheels. But there's something worse yet: those familiar little 67-liter recycling boxes that leave the streets strewn with paper, cans, and plastic. A pox on our city. Until these abominations were discontinued, the City of Montreal used to claim they were "keeping our public spaces cleaner." Dream on.

The giant wheelie bins are the most widely used recycling containers. That doesn't mean they're necessarily the best, especially in winter. On a snow-covered sidewalk, they won't budge; they're too bulky to pull between two parked cars; they get stuck in ice crusts on the way to the truck. And wrestling with a giant bin like that makes it far too easy to graze or hit a vehicle. For all these reasons, a shift on recycling is a surefire recipe for a day of bellyaching. I know, I hear you: garbagemen will spend their days whining and bitching no matter what shift they're on. Fair enough. But put a garbageman on recycling, especially in winter, and prepare to hear the drawn-out lamentations of a cursed soul.

Long story short, picking up recycling bins in NDG in winter is no fun, to put it mildly. And there's no shortage of residents along the route who think they're hot shit. One day, I was on recycling in NDG, scrambling between the garbage bins askew in the snow and the recycling bins I had to lift onto the truck. After emptying one green bin, as I was trying to catch my breath, I tossed the bin back as best I could without getting behind. The route was a real obstacle course that day. I caught a glimpse of a guy staring at me, very close, with deep disapproval in his eyes. I returned his stare and asked him what was up.

"You could try being a bit more careful with the bins!"

At that moment, something came over me, so strong I couldn't control it. Usually, I just try to ignore the many snotty comments that come our way in the course of our day. I've learned from experience that nothing positive ever comes from answering. But this time . . .

"I'm doing my best. The snow wasn't shoveled, so I can't work properly. If you're not happy, complain! I'd love to get taken off your route, with these conditions. Any time!"

And that's when he dares to say it.

"You chose your job. Quit whining."

I felt like asking him if he said dumb shit like that to his girlfriend when she complained about him: "You chose me, quit whining." Instead, I tried to take a more diplomatic tack.

"Why don't you come out and try working in this snow for a day. I'd like to see if you'd still file a complaint after that. Yeah, I chose my job. But I didn't choose my conditions."

"I went to school so I wouldn't have to do a job like that. Try getting an education."

Shiiiii . . . Talk about symbolic violence. Pierre Bourdieu must be turning over in his grave. How cute, this upstanding taxpayer is telling me to change careers! He's only just met me. Bold move. I couldn't resist telling him I had a master's degree. It's not something I usually like talking about in front of the other guys, but then . . . Surprised and suddenly interested, the guy asked me what I was doing picking up garbage. And then he left. I don't think he ever believed me about my education.

It reminds me of the mother of a friend of mine, who also has a university degree and who I brought into the garbage business. She was also constantly on him to quit. And of course, I've heard the same thing myself, plenty of times. Why should I quit? So someone else can do this tough, thankless, but essential job? To leave it exclusively to the ones who lost the lottery of life? But when I stop and think about it, I can't say for sure why I insist on being a garbage collector in the first place. Maybe it's a vocation? In any case, I take a lot of pride in how my daily work keeps our cities clean. And I feel solidarity with all the people working behind the scenes, whose anonymous labor lets all of us enjoy a better life. *Those* are people I respect. And it could be plain old-fashioned pride or my combative instincts at work: I'm determined to prove that no job is "lower" than another.

Certainly, that's what I'd like to get across to this neighborhood resident. But he'd rather turn his back to me than listen to me. There is a handful of very simple, tiny truths that scare good middle-class citizens half to death.

GARBAGE DOESN'T LIE (III)

GREEN BINS

Every week you see them lined up on the roadside, silent but full of hope and pride: a battalion of green 240-liter rolling bins. They know that they're the foot soldiers on the front lines of an epic battle. Just imagine it. Every year on planet Earth, four hundred million tons of plastic are produced. Huge amounts of that are dumped into the ocean. It washes up in the sea, sticks to rock formations, and even coats them in a sort of plastic crust.[8] This plastic surgery is detrimental to the mollusks, which are poisoned. And then there's the rest: paper, aluminum, and glass. It adds up to tons upon tons of waste.

For good, tax-paying citizens, the 240-liter green wheelie bin is the front line in the battle to stem this tide of recyclables. The green bin embodies the promise of victory in the war against pollution.

We garbagemen see something different.

My efforts collecting recyclables in green bins reassures good consumers by creating the illusion that the planet is safe and sound. Recycling is a magic trick, or more properly a sleight of hand. The garbageman makes all your paper and plastic disappear—tadaaa!—and at the same time they cleanse our guilty middle-class consciences. In Europe, the biggest producers and consumers of plastic are the Germans, who also happen to be the recycling champions. Plastic consumption and recycling go hand in hand. We all want to live under the illusion that all the plastic we dispose of gets recycled, but the truth is that the real figure is just 10 percent. The rest is shipped out of our sight to poorer countries or ends up in the ocean, where we have literally created an entire new continent of plastic.

What's the solution? Unquestionably we have to consume as little as possible. All nonessential uses of plastic should be banned. Unfortunately, 98 percent of single-use plastic products are made from fossil fuels. Big Oil stands firm against any reduction in plastics production.[9] And so do the national governments of petrostates.

We have all seen the ridiculous heights that this pro-plastic stance can reach. In Canada, Pierre Poilievre, who is a member of parliament and the leader of the Conservative Party, as well as an unabashed champion of oil companies, has made the right to use plastic straws a national priority.[10] Oh, I'm sure the Conservative Party leader recycles his straws. But the raw materials that go into the recycling process are often soiled, marred with toxins, and otherwise unrecoverable. An investigative report on Quebec television found that one company, Ricova, sent batches of contaminated recyclable materials to India.[11] Since Ricova operates in Montreal, we're talking about recyclables I picked up with my own two hands. Recyclables that you took care to wash and sort, and on whose behalf extra trucks were sent out on the roads, burning fossil fuels, not to mention all the other inputs in the production chain.

Even when they aren't contaminated, our recyclable waste still often ends up on the other side of the world. In Asia, milk bags and yogurt containers from Quebec are piling up into small mountains. Women and children sort through these plastics to reuse a small fraction while the rest degrades in the soil or is burned up in furnaces by unscrupulous operators, sending toxic smoke billowing into the sky. Make no mistake: the contents of our green bins poison the water, soil, and air of Indians and Indonesians, impacting human health.[12] Chinese firms, which are better organized and more prudent, began turning away our recyclable waste in 2017, for reasons including its poor quality.

Anthropologist Mikaëla Le Meur describes the work of the Vietnamese women in the town of Minh Khai whose job it is to unpack the bales of plastic that arrive by shipping containers from across the world.[13] These women must work bent over in unhealthy postures, for ten hours a day, doing the dirty work that cleans up the filth produced for and by the rich of our world.

"Does this job exist in other countries?" one worker asked Le Meur.

"No, I don't think so," she answered.

"Then take me with you to France," the old woman replied.

On a global scale, what distinguishes rich from poor is that one group has the privilege of getting rid of their waste, while the other group inherits it, as anthropologist Ambre Fourrier has pointed out.[14] The garbage collector is somewhere in the middle of this spectrum.

I often think that if instead of sending our waste across the ocean we had to pile it up on Mount Royal in Montreal or Central Park in New York City, the Pierre Poilievres and Donald Trumps of the world might just get used to drinking without straws. Maybe.

RECYCLING

What's in a word?

The word *recycling* may be older than you think: it was first used in the oil industry in the 1920s to describe the process of returning production residues into the refinery process.[15] Only much later, in the 1960s and 1970s, did the word acquire its current meaning. On May 22, 1970, the first Earth Day, the Möbius strip was adopted as the logo for recycling: a loop with no beginning or end, symbolizing the desire for freedom from waste.

Of the famous three *R*s—reduce, reuse, and recycle—the first commandment always gets short shrift. Waste management companies have no idea what to do with the first *R*, which horrifies them since their entire development model is based on revenue growth. The second *R*, *reuse*, also isn't part of their business model. Some waste management companies even have regulations forbidding garbagemen from keeping items they find in the course of their work.

The industry is far more enthusiastic about recycling. It's the only socially acceptable solution, because it allows the waste business to keep growing. Industrial society is selling us a utopia: the notion that increased production can result in less waste. More crap, less waste: that's the plan, folks. No wonder recycling takes up so much space.

A SORTING CENTER

Wherever I turn my head, I see mind-boggling heaps of garbage. I'm at Tiru, a recycling center in Montreal's

Saint-Michel district. My coworker Stéphane had warned me—"Tiru's a helluva mess!" I see what he meant.

"Is that recycling or garbage? Or do they do both here?" I ask him now.

There's glass all over the place, seagulls perched on bales, and the whole site is so cluttered that vehicles can barely get around. Trucks are driving on a layer of loose waste, crushing it. While I get that this is a waste management site, even for a dump, it's utter chaos. It feels like we're at serious risk of going up in flames at any moment. The City must be worried.

"None of this even looks like recycling," says Stéphane. "Sometimes it takes three or four hours to offload. We just dump shit anywhere. There's more and more of it coming in every day. But it's like nothing ever leaves!"

No one used to be concerned about the absurdity of this landscape. That changed quickly when China stopped buying our recycling due to its poor quality. Since recycling is sold by weight, it wasn't uncommon for the bales they bought from Western countries to be laced with heavier materials, like bricks and concrete, an underhanded way to boost its value. The government acted surprised. But to anyone on the ground, it's long been obvious that things aren't going well at all.

A PHONE CALL

I place a call to an official of a government-funded Quebec e-waste recycling organization, the Association pour le recyclage des produits électroniques (Electronic Products Recycling Association), or ARPE.

"I'm calling to share my concerns," I explain. "I'm a garbage collector. And I want to let you know about something I've been noticing out in the field. In Montreal North, where I'm working now, we pick up around four CRT TVs every day. And there are thirteen trucks out in the area. So if we assume that all of those trucks are carrying four TVs, that means that fifty-two TVs are being thrown out every day, just in Montreal North. If we then do the math and think about the entire province of Quebec, that's a lot of TVs we're talking about, right? Ten, twenty thousand, or even more."

"No, that's impossible," the man answers.

Well, he'd know.

Since that time, not a day has gone by when I haven't tossed at least one plasma TV into the hopper. The plastic clatters into the truck's belly with a thud.

When I was young, our teachers used to ask us how many TV sets we had at home. Owning multiple TVs was a status symbol. One in every room wasn't unheard of. Multiplied by every household in Quebec, that's a lot of TVs that need to get tossed out sooner or later! And whenever a new technology comes out, that'll be the same number again that we'll then have to buy all over again—and again, and again, for every new technology cycle.

Of course, TVs are nothing special. It's the same story with every technology. Go shopping for lights at any hardware store and the associates will recommend one of the new-style fixtures made with LED mini-light strips. They generally come with a twenty-thousand-hour guarantee. It sounds like a lot, right? But then what? At that point, they always get slightly embarrassed. "Well, then you replace it!" The second I hear that, I see the writing on the wall: any week now I'm going to be picking up all kinds of LED light fixtures.

I'm still on the phone with the e-waste organization. I'm thinking that I may have gotten through to one of the few people who might actually be in a position to do something about the massive amounts of crap I have to collect every day on the truck. *Don't give up on him so fast!* I tell myself.

"Yes . . . But listen, I've started opening up the TVs to pull out the copper and the wiring. But I know that it's still releasing mercury into the atmosphere . . . And I don't see any other solutions."

And the gentleman's very candid answer was: "Please, don't do that. It's bad for the environment. Thank you."

And then he hung up.

ABOLISH WINTER!

After a snowstorm, Montreal is a completely different city: cleaner, quieter, less gray. It looks peaceful and pure. Nature envelops the whole city in a thick, cozy blanket of white that reflects the sun's rays back on us with a brightness that makes it feel like some kind of paradise. Just the day before, it was the usual asphalt and concrete.

The breathtaking beauty of this spectacle puts me in a foul mood. I already know I'm going to be stuck out there working in a foot of snow. And it just keeps coming down. On social media, the enchanting photos of perky city dwellers gliding through the streets on their cross-country skis are racking up the likes and little hearts—but we don't get to pick up the garbage on skis or skates, or ride around in sleds. We have to trudge along on our own two feet. And putting one foot in front of the other in fresh snow is a pain in the ass. I'm sinking, the snow's working its way into my boots, every footstep is hard work, and I spend the whole day wondering whether this load is the one that's going to make me slip and fall flat on my back with my arms and legs in the air and a nice pile of garbage on my stomach. The whole thing is preposterous.

And it's only going to get worse. In winter conditions, I can't even drag the wheelie bins. I have to grab them in a bear hug, haul them over, and then lift them over the snowbanks that have cropped up everywhere. Then, once I do manage to get the thing over to the truck—it's the size of a small fridge—I have to hold it up and keep it in balance, so the truck's mechanical arms can pick it up and empty it out.

Honestly, hauling recycling in winter should be an

Olympic sport. Up right after the moguls: a new race where elite athletes haul 240-liter recycling bins over and across the snowbanks.

Here's a sneak preview, based on my own workday in the snow. First, I have to break away from the truck as fast as possible. Next, I clear the first obstacle—a classic snowbank spilling over on each side of a parked car. Oh, and the said car is parked in a trench shoveled out by its owner, with high walls of snow on either side. Once that first obstacle is cleared, I have to leap over the snowdrift onto the edge of the sidewalk, for the weightlifting part of the event: lift the overstuffed garbage bin stuck in the resident's snowbank. Note that the snow is likely packed tightly enough to form a crust over the outside and the inside of the bin, weighing it down. Wrestle it free and drag it to the truck—all while maintaining a pace that can keep me hoping to finish my route the same day I started it. That's a lot of snowbanks on every route!

All this winter-wonderland business is a royal waste of our time. On garbage routes, it costs us at least an hour per truckload; on recycling, even more. When the snow plows have to go by, people can't put their big bins out on the sidewalk. Of course, they're going to pull out all the stops to get their bins out, come hell or high water. How many times has an upstanding taxpayer left their bin perched precariously on top of a giant mountain of snow? And needless to say, people generally can't be bothered to clear the snow and ice from their bin lids. I know what they're thinking: we have to empty it out anyway, may as well get a two-for-one, at no extra charge. These are exactly the kind of good middle-class people who religiously shovel every inch of their driveways and balconies. And it goes without saying that they never fail to clear off their precious automobiles. But the lowly recycling bin? Never. Everything on the property is clean as a goddamn whistle, crisp as freshly ironed laundry—everything except the garbage cans, which are left covered in layers of slush, ice, and snow. Why bother? It's the garbageman's problem, right? Do dukes and duchesses clean out their valets' closets?

A major snowstorm is a three-day affair: The day of the storm itself; the following day, when we're in the thick of it; and the day after as well. For at least three days, everything slows to a crawl. For us, that means three days of tromping through snowbanks chasing your trash. It doesn't take a city-planning genius to see that something is wrong here.

In Morocco, when it gets too hot, productive activities requiring heavy physical effort are postponed until evening. Couldn't Quebec have a similar rule? When the accumulation of snow is more than six inches, put off garbage collection! Just one thing: The guys still get paid. In recognition of the work we do throughout the year.

Before the snow is scraped and collected, all it takes is one cold day for everything to freeze. Now, you're climbing mountains of ice and running on slippery, uneven surfaces, and unemptied garbage cans are frozen into the ground and jammed stiff. Slow going for sure, and bloody dangerous too. Worst of all is the usual smarty-pants who balances their garbage can, bag, and—why not?—bin on the summit of an ice-covered Mount Everest. I can guarantee you that's one garbage can I *am* going to put back *exactly* where I found it.

If at least there was some kind of recognition—a bonus, a vacation, anything to get us through this punishing time of year. It wouldn't cost a fortune. There aren't that many storms every year, and thanks to global warming we can expect even fewer in the future. But clearly that's too much to ask. The top minds always have more important things to worry about. Laws regulating the color of margarine. People hunting deer in parks. Or how about the project to build a bridge between Quebec City and Lévis, a promise they have been holding out to the public for decades without anything happening. The latest incarnation calls for the third bridge to be built next to the *two* we have already. Apparently, bridges win elections.

Perhaps the reason it's so critical to collect the trash without delay, rain or shine and sleet or snow, is that someone, somewhere, is worried that if you give garbagemen an extra day off, they might get a taste for rest. They'll go soft. Could it be that it simply never occurred to the people making decisions that there are certain weather conditions where we can just put garbage collection on hold? I guess that's inconceivable.

But one day some official in their office *did* take the time to invent rules to punish me if, by some misfortune, after emptying an icy bin into the garbage truck, I put it back in a way where it so much as touches the sidewalk. It's inane. You don't want to postpone collection on icy days when the truck is still twenty-five feet ahead when it brakes. Taking out your household garbage on the day of a snowstorm is so important, so crucial, it's as if that act alone might protect us from the chaos of the snow.

It reminds me of the day a supervisor for one company, Matrec, came to see me in the midst of an honest-to-god snowstorm. He wanted to warn me to put the garbage cans back "properly." Let's say the man's timing left something to be desired. In a storm, you're always a hair closer to breaking your neck than at any other time. In this job, the pressure of keeping up always runs high, but now it's overflowing. It's not just performance that's at stake; you also feel you have to do more than usual. Garbagemen are strong guys, so of course we're expected to help push stuck cars out of snowbanks. But then again, when I do help rescue a fellow citizen in this way, I put myself in the path of the shower of insults from all the drivers who have to wait because they're stuck behind the garbage truck.

Let's get back to the crux of the matter: bin placement. In a storm, the City asks residents not to place their bins in the street or on the sidewalk. Remember that, especially with recycling bins, we're handling massive containers that can weigh up to two-hundred pounds, in two feet of snow. Even emptied, we're still talking fifteen to twenty pounds to drag through two feet of hard-packed, bumpy snow. As if that weren't enough, there's the sidewalk plow: we can't have bins in its path. The driveway curb isn't an option, since it's been taken over by the snow, and the homeowner will scream bloody murder if you put the bin in the path of his car. And while we're on the topic of the car, let's not forget that its window is fogged up and it's covered in snow, making it all-too-likely that it's going to cut off or even slam into our garbage truck. You can't see it coming, with snow in your eyes, but you can sure feel them crunching. Pressure is rising all around us. I swear, there are days when it feels as if a sophisticated conspiracy has been orchestrated against you and the entire city is in on it.

And that's when the supervisor—you know, the guy who should be bringing you coffee, patting you on the back for being out there on the front lines, thanking you for your dedication—that's when he decides to come over and tell me to do a better job of positioning my garbage cans. I look at him, give him a universal sign to fuck off, and then heave the garbage can into the resident's yard.

Now, this particular move, which may seem unreasonable to you, dear reader, is actually often the best course of action in stormy weather. The garbage can is placed on the property, doesn't interfere with municipal or private snow-removal services, and remains accessible to the good citizen. Win-win, for homeowner and garbageman—but still maybe not the best move to pull in front of a supervisor you've just told to fuck off

What's the root cause of all this strife? The human-centered ethos of modernity. Ever since Descartes and his successors decided to put humanity at the center of the world, we've believed that it makes sense to vanquish the forces of nature. We think we can beat winter. No snowstorm is going to stop a virtuous tax-payer from leaving their half-empty recycling bin by the side of the road! But when you're the one picking up this garbage in the middle of a snowstorm, when you're up to your neck in winter, it doesn't take long to realize that the idea of being stronger than nature is a load of crap

"Abolish winter!" was the rallying cry of the Quebec anthropologist Bernard Arcand. He understood that living here, it makes more sense to slow down in January and February than to stubbornly keep trying to domesticate the snow and cold. Amen, brother.

HEAT WAVE

The heat wave sets in. A huge pocket of suffocating humidity is holding our little corner of the planet in its death grip. I think of the lyrics of what might be Quebec's most iconic song, Gilles Vigneault's "Mon pays": "My country is not a country, it's winter."[16] Well, from where I'm standing, that's hard to imagine. My country is a tropical republic, a sauna, a furnace, an outpost of hell.

When the heat wave strikes, you start checking the weather every day, the same way you check for snowstorms in mid-January. You read the weather advisories—stay inside, avoid the sun, limit physical exertion to a strict minimum. Sounds nice, right? But is there a way to collect the trash while staying home and not moving? Nope. I'm cooked, more or less literally.

Every heat wave triggers anxiety attacks so intense that the only thing that gets me through is my overdeveloped desire to push myself to new feats of endurance. I know I'm going to have to work just as hard, whatever the conditions. And the garbage isn't going to wait for the heat to break. Doing this job means going out, time and again, and conquering nature—both actual temperatures and precipitation, and my own personal weather. But whenever a heat wave comes on, the challenge is especially harrowing.

My misgivings are based on hard-won personal experience. I vividly remember getting so dehydrated that I cramped up for the entire return trip home after work. I had to stop halfway home, unable to finish my drive. My body was as parched as the Sahara Desert. Going another inch without stopping to hydrate myself was inconceivable. When you get to the end of a day like that, a heavy anxiety descends. And you know you'll have to go out and do the same thing the very next day.

How do I do it? I need to maximize recovery time, just to be able to get up and go to work again. Eat, sleep, drink lots of fluids, make sure the next day is no more excruciating than the last. It's stressful! You're used to being indestructible, unkillable. You're the guy who springs right back—but now your head is heavy, you feel as if your body is at its breaking point, the machine's basic functions are jamming up. Muscles, joints, flesh: Nothing is following orders anymore. It's like a general strike has paralyzed your body. An insurrection in the ranks.

When dehydration sets in, you don't feel thirsty, but you have to drink; you don't feel hungry, but you have to eat. By the time your appetite returns, it's bedtime already: too late. You have to sleep, but the burns on your skin and the sweat oozing from your body turn your bed itself into another sworn enemy. It feels as if your body is screaming at you, as if no matter what you do—drinking, eating, resting—it's the *exact* opposite of what you should be doing! But you have no choice. So you have to calculate the costs and benefits of satisfying each of your physiological needs. Eat, drink, sleep. A little, a lot? When, how? This heat wave drags you deep into the inner folds of your being, where you experience a level of wretchedness you are wholly unaccustomed to.

"Ooooh, that stinks" is the single most common thing you hear as a garbageman. "You must get dirty" is a close second. The implication, sometimes left tacit and sometimes made explicit, is that *you* stink, and *you* are inherently unclean. Our answer, if we haven't given up on answering such a stupid question altogether, is something along the lines of "I take a shower when I finish work, just like everyone else!"

Let's talk smells, though. Riding behind a garbage truck is a bit like being on a farm. After a while you stop smelling anything at all. There are exceptions, of course. One garbageman trainer I know, Nicker, had a helper who would throw up when he reached the end of the first street on the route. After that, he was fine. And I knew another helper who would actually spray perfume into the hopper, which makes about as much sense as trying to empty out a lake with a ladle. For most of us, though, the smell just goes away.

We know that thousands of people lived in medieval towns that were basically open-air sewers. Compared to that, a garbage truck is a rose garden. And here's a strange confession: when it's my day off, I often actually find myself taking pleasure in the waft of a distant garbage truck as I go about my "civilian" business.

That said, things change during heat waves. And that's when there's some truth in what people say: no matter how many times I try to wash my hands, they still smell. And when the city starts to swelter, you've got another problem on your hands: grubs. Organic matter attracts flies looking for good places to lay their eggs. The heat accelerates their reproductive cycle. Before you know it, white worms are wriggling and swarming in every garbage bag and along the walls and floors and underlids of every trash can. At this point, there are only two attitudes to adopt. One is to just stop caring. The other is to try to manipulate the trash bags in a way that directs the countless worms coming out of and off them away from you. You don't want this invasion of soft little critters to spill over onto your body, to the point where you find them in your shoes at night and feel them writhing up into your arm hair or, worse, wriggling around in the hair on your head. I'm not squeamish, but that's plain gross.

So we're mired in a heat wave. After running just two hundred yards, you are drenched in sweat. You have to drink nonstop, pace yourself like a marathon runner, monitor your energy expenditure—but you also have to screen out some of the messages your body is sending you, without totally ignoring them either. Dirt and dust are clinging to you, but they're also washed away by the sweat that beads up on your body. As it dries, it leaves a thin crust of salt on your face. And these successive waves of sweat don't stop once the work is done. After all, your body is generating them in an attempt to lower your internal temperature.

On days like these, you're not exactly at your best.

Yet despite this torment, I still find a way to love the heat. It's just one more challenge, and challenges drive me.

For new guys, though, heat waves can be deadly. I remember my first experience of heatstroke, one of my first shifts working in Kirkland. I'd started my day normally, without giving the heat too much thought. I seemed to be going along as usual when, without really understanding, I felt ill. I started throwing up on the sprawling lawn, grass of a green so bright it really brought out the contrast with what I was throwing down. I was dazed, stunned. No idea if the homeowner ever saw me. No one stepped in. Without any clear sense of what was going on, I kept going . . . only to tell the driver that I couldn't keep going. A shameful moment.

He dropped me off at a gas station on Highway 40. The company's responsibility ended there. Crouching on the floor between the washrooms and the garbage can, I threw up everything I had left over from the previous day's lunch and dinner, to the indifference of everyone passing me by. Maybe they'd mistaken me for a homeless person? Then again, they were few and far between on the wealthy West Island of Montreal. I just stayed there, slumped over, unable to move. After a while, having regained enough strength to get up, I walked up to the gas station counter and asked the clerk if I could use the phone. I called my mom. She couldn't come herself and had to send my grandfather.

It took a few years, but my mom has come to accept that I'm a garbageman. I think she likes that I earn a good living. I've studied psychology, and management too. I could work in a crisis center, or your run-of-the-mill office. And I bet my mom has imagined me doing all these different jobs. But she respects the one I have. She still doesn't like talking about it overmuch. And I think that's because she can never quite forget about some of the bad days, like the one when I got heatstroke and she had to send my grandfather to the rescue.

Or my third day at work as a garbageman. What a disaster. In Mirabel, I slipped off the running board and set my foot down on the ground instead of bringing it back up like I should have. The traction of the road and the speed of the truck threw my body into the air. I rolled face first onto the hot asphalt. When the driver saw me lying inert in his mirror, he thought I was dead. My mom came to pick me up from the clinic. Once I got home, I took the most painful shower of my life. My mom still remembers my screams. For her, that's what it means for her son to be a garbageman. And I can imagine that every time there's a heat wave, she must get a little worried too.

SEE LORRAINE AND DIE

It's spring, 2012, in Lorraine, a northern suburb of Montreal.

Now, Lorraine is a lovely place, a peaceful community where good upstanding taxpayers can put the troubles of the world behind them in the comfort of their bungalows. Working here fills me with idyllic feelings, what with all the trees and greenery, all that clean fresh air. The yards are gorgeous, the streets wide and clear—and did I mention just how green it is? There are roundabouts for traffic-calming, parks aplenty, and smart land-use planning that creates areas where cars are out of the way and our trucks can drive along in peace. Since there's no industry in Lorraine, we rarely have to deal with other trucks on the road.

I'm in Lorraine to cover a shift for Édouard, a tall, slim guy who carries himself with pride and is always happy to take off his shirt and show off his body. One remarkable thing about Édouard is that he always has a smile on his face—a rare trait in a garbageman. Of course, that doesn't stop him from yelling at drivers who get too close. But there's something about him, the look in his eye, the way he carries himself, his entire physique—everything about him tells you you're in the presence of a man with a healthy sense of self-respect, a man who won't let anyone push him around. I remember the first time we worked together. I'd earned a reputation as a formidable helper, a guy who could throw more than my fair share of trash. Édouard knew it, and I'd heard rumors he was planning to see if he could burn me out, starting the moment I got behind a truck with him. You see, running behind a garbage truck isn't just a job, it's also a game. So once Édouard and I found each other, we had plenty of fun pushing our limits together. And he pushed me pretty hard. But he never burned me out.

Back then, Édouard was one of the few Black garbagemen in the business in Quebec. It's not like the United States, or France, where most garbagemen are Black, and many are immigrants. In Quebec in 2012, the world of garbage was still a pretty white one.

Today, it's a different story. Where I work, around one in three garbagemen no longer shares my background. These changes haven't always been seamless. Garbagemen rarely play nice, and we often talk to each other in crude, stupid, nasty terms, usually without a second thought. I'm not going to lie: sometimes the foul language used is downright racist, in the mouths of white people.

I once asked a Black garbageman I'm close to if the racially charged language affected him. He told me he didn't mind—except for one time, when a foreman from a large company called out to him: "Hey, *le bronzé*!" (which literally means "tanned," but you get the idea). It pissed my friend off that a boss, who was above him in the power structure, would demean him with disrespectful words. But otherwise, he says, he doesn't mind. That may be.

I am convinced that running side by side behind a garbage truck flattens out ethnic differences. We are truly all the same before the load to be lifted, bound tightly together by the task at hand. When you're throwing trash, only one thing matters: getting that garbage out of the way. And the job requires the close collaboration of newbies and vets, runners and drivers, the fastest and the most agile of us. The work instills a genuine sense of solidarity.

And I'd go a step further. In my view, everyone knows that everyone picking up garbage—Black, Latino, or those labeled as "white trash"—are all basically poor people. Our brotherhood is a gathering of marginal deviants, antisocial conspiracy theorists, eccentrics, and others who have a hard time fully integrating into the "straight world." This outsider status forges our identity as garbagemen. Sure, we could turn it into a misery contest, argue about who has truly suffered the most and had the hardest time of it, remark how even on the margins we're not truly equal—but that's really more of an academic game than what we garbagemen spend our time worrying about.

The reason I've been called in to work for Édouard is because he's injured. And in Lorraine, he warns me, "they treat us like dogs." The loads are heavy and we have to pick up the "green"—piles of branches, mounds of grass clippings, dead leaves, tall mountains of organic waste. Life in the suburbs is heavy. It got to be too much for Édouard. In addition to being a royal pain in his ass, it did a number on his back.

These were the days before brown plastic compost bins. So suburbanites emptied out their grass clippings, weeds, and branches in oversized bags. Full to the brim. The sheer size and weight of those piles of bags is barely conceivable. For starters, they're often too heavy to quickly pick up and toss into the truck. You have to use both hands to grab the bag, press it against the back of the truck, and then shove it over the lip into the hopper. Garden waste piles up at the bottom of the leaf bags, which are made of paper, causing them to get unbalanced and easily tear when overloaded. Such, such were the joys.

Why is it, you may ask, that we have so much green "waste" in the first place? Because beauty comes at a price. Trees, landscaping, large flowerbeds, gardens—all this organic life produces fruit, plant waste, and broken branches. Nature decomposes, it putrefies, it's muddy. It's dirty. But model citizens aren't having any of it. They want to live in a controlled, sanitized, smoothed-out environment. They want to live in a magazine ad. Not surrounded by piles of decomposing leaves.

The yards in Lorraine range in size from large to immense. Of course, the homeowners often hire out their yardwork to landscaping services. From what I can see, the landscapers are working up a storm: planting, pruning, and mowing without respite. In any event, they're creating mountains of green waste. And it falls to us garbagemen to dispose of it all in the end.

Once collected, this residue gets dropped off at Compost Ste-Anne, a social economy enterprise. Their employees, who are mostly of Latin American origin, open up the residents' plastic bags to pull out the contents. That's the way our system works: Underpaid immigrants handle the composting in upscale suburbs. And in return, these suburbanites get free bags of compost, proof positive that they are doing their part to save the planet.

This compost drop-off center is right next to Lorraine, at the Sainte-Anne-des-Plaines prison. I guess *those* residents are in no position to complain about the smell. This proximity to the landfill has an impact on the intensity of the work. Once it's unloaded, the truck can move through the streets more quickly. This speeds up the pace and boosts our daily tonnage. The pace of work is frantic, and the weight of the garbage is insane.

In Lorraine, all the conditions are in place for a guy to get injured. Even a big and tough guy like Édouard.

MY FIRST DAY IN ÉDOUARD'S boots is memorable. We start off in the higher elevations of this small town. There isn't much to pick up, but what little there is here is heavy as hell! When we get to the end of the road, we find a house that's pushing its luck about as far as it will go. They are far, far over the collection limit. I decide to leave the leaf-filled garbage cans uncollected. It's not really my style—but fuck it, a line has been crossed.

An older fellow is sitting out on the deck, giving off serious frustrated bougie vibes. I can see him staring at me out of the corner of my eye. He wants to make sure I "do my job." Even if he doesn't carry out his end of the bargain. I can tell what he's thinking: "I pay my taxes, don't I? This service is owed to me." In his mind, if something doesn't get picked up, I'm to blame. There's no room for discussion. He's watching me. He sees that I'm checking out his garbage cans of leaves, and that there's a chance I'm going to leave them there. He sidles over. I stop. Time stands still. My driver, Paul, comes over to see what's going on.

What a colossal waste of time!

And in this job, there's no time to waste. A garbage truck is out of place in small communities like this. The noise of the hydraulic compression system, the roar of its twelve-ton engine, the heat emanating from its all-metal chassis, the smell of the load, the danger it represents due to its power, weight, and size, its dirtiness, the filth of the garbagemen riding on the running boards . . . none of this fits into the bucolic surroundings of affluent suburbs. Local residents, drivers, delivery people—everyone who sees a garbage truck pull up is thinking the same thing: "I want this business out of the way as soon as possible!" All the sources of pressure that we feel constantly. The driver feels trapped in the narrow streets, sandwiched between the cars passing him on the side or impatiently stuck behind us in the rear. As for us, we're racing through these cars, ready to run over anything in our way just to squeeze into the smallest space that opens up in front of them. We're right in the middle of traffic, but we're moving at the wrong pace.

No one ever stops to think about how the tiny slowdown we occasion for them is in fact saving *them* time. That by taking care of their waste for them, we free them up to focus on other things. That, knowing this as they do, they could just chill the fuck out and wait for us to finish.

Long story short, when Paul the driver stops his truck and gets out of his cab to assess the situation, it means the situation is serious. He had sensed that the man coming over to me was looking for trouble. Maybe he was worried we might come to blows? It's not uncommon for a garbageman to hit a customer. But that's not really my style either. I even decide to pick up his goddamned 120-pound garbage cans, filled with leaves and grass mixed with crushed stone (what else?). I have to shake them hard to get the contents to empty into the tank. As I do so, I turn to the man and yell:

"Gee, you ever think about making the load a little lighter? You know, think about us?"

"Your job's not so hard. Quit whining. I could handle it myself."

I stop for a moment and look him up and down. We're talking about an older gentleman—he must be about seventy. He's getting quite skinny, so that even if he was in good shape at one time, I still seriously doubt what he's saying.

"Okay, great. I'll set it up. A day on the truck, we can work together. You'd do that, hey?"

"Any time. I'll show you," replies this arrogant fuck.

Our conversation takes place as the driver and I are struggling to lift his garbage cans—of course he isn't deigning to help. Because yes, it took two of us to lift each can. And this old bastard can't even be bothered to thank us. I'm in shock. When it's all over, I sit up front with Paul (in green waste runs, the pickups are often so far away that helpers sit in the cab . . . and anyway, I had some venting to do).

"Come the fuck on, he can't be serious," I say. "I'll talk to Bobby [the dispatcher] tomorrow. If I can spend a day with the guy, he'll see what it's like. Fuckhead."

Paul is calmer, and makes me see reason.

"Simon, if you do that, you'll end up killing the old guy."

Which is exactly what the dispatcher said—word for word—when I asked him the next day.

Too bad!

SPEAKING OF GRUMPY OLD BASTARDS, on the day I write down the story of my attempt to bring an old guy on the truck for a day, I come across a column by right-wing pundit Mathieu Bock-Côté, who happens to be a proud son of the same suburb, Lorraine. Bock-Côté lives in Paris now, where he's pursuing a dazzling career as a rent-a-quote pontificator in a tailored suit. Now, in the spring of 2023, France is in the midst of a pension reform crisis, and the garbage collectors have decided to stop picking up the garbage. "It's a scandal!" exclaims Quebec's favorite suburbanite-turned-dandy.

Bock-Côté, of course, calls for an end to this "madness." How? By thinking a little less about the rights of the strikers and more about "the right to have an urban environment where filth doesn't pile up." Of course, there's not one word about the reason for the dispute, which is about recognizing the "arduous nature of the work of sanitation professionals"—hardly the type of work that can be performed until age sixty-five. The worker's suffering is the last concern for this self-satisfied champion of petit bourgeois values. As for the right to *not* be confronted with the consequences of all the shit he produces and consumes—*that* is sacred.

I've never met a garbageman from Lorraine. So I'm happy to extend the offer I made to the gentleman with the trash cans full of rocks to Mathieu Bock-Côté as well: Come spend a day behind a garbage truck, as a worthy representative of your hometown, and of your social class. As a sociologist, you'll surely understand the value and appreciate the experience of doing some fieldwork. And once you've done that, let me know if you feel any differently about the situation.

But perhaps our eminent pundit just doesn't have the time for such an experiment. Instead, let me propose a thought experiment, an exercise in sociological thinking. Imagine, for a moment, what would happen if our society decided to accord status to jobs based on their social utility or necessity. And that to establish this hierarchy of value, this scale of social status, we ask ourselves the following question: What would happen if the group in question stopped working? Would we collectively suffer if corporate lawyers went on strike? Would panic take hold if advertising conceptors stopped concepting? Could we live without nurses or teachers longer than real estate developers? And, I ask you, Mr. Bock-Côté: Would a strike of newspaper columnists plunge society into an existential crisis?

The historian Rutger Bregman reminds us that when New York garbagemen went on strike in 1968, ten thousand tons of garbage piled up on the streets of Gotham every day! Rats had the run of the town, the air grew rank, and everyone feared for public health. The authorities declared a state of emergency. As often happens, the army was called in to pick up the trash as the strike wore on. After ten days, the City agreed to the workers' demands.

Bregman draws our attention to the fact that at the same time as the New York garbage strike, bank employees in Ireland were on strike as well. That strike lasted *six months*, without any apparent negative impact on the economy, emergency legislation, or major embarrassments. Bregman concludes that, by the logic of utility, garbagemen should earn more than bankers.

Another historic garbage strike occurred in 1968

in Memphis, Tennessee. This one was even bigger than New York. Ninety percent of garbagemen in Memphis were Black. Throughout the South, garbage collection was often considered a job too lowly for white men. And conditions in Memphis were bad: The garbagemen wore dirty clothes, handling metal trash cans with jagged bits that cut them and holes that sprayed them with garbage juice. They worked long hours with no paid vacation and no sick leave. Their pay was so low that even a full-time garbageman could still qualify for social assistance!

The spark that set off the dispute was a tragic event on February 1, 1968: Echol Cole (36) and Robert Walker (30) were killed in the line of duty. A violent storm struck Memphis that day. Prevented by Jim Crow laws from sheltering in a building along their route, the two men took refuge in the only place they could: the hopper of their garbage truck. Tragedy struck when someone accidentally activated the compactor. They were crushed.

The 1968 Memphis garbage strike began on February 12 and ended on April 16 in victory for the strikers. But at what price? By February 15, thousands of tons of garbage were cluttering up the city, and polite society was revolted. The garbage collectors, rallying under the slogan "I am a man," clashed with the police. On March 18, Martin Luther King Jr. came to Memphis to support the workers, as part of the Poor People's Campaign. On March 28, Dr. King took part in a demonstration that degenerated into a riot. A sixteen-year-old was killed by the police, around 60 people were injured, and 280 were arrested. All the ingredients for a social explosion converged—economic injustice, racism, and the struggle for civil rights. Conservatives, as you can imagine, grumbled about this disturbance to the social order.

Martin Luther King returned to Memphis in support of the sanitation workers. On April 3, he gave one of his most famous speeches, "I've Been to the Mountaintop," in which he repeated the cry of Black Americans, of poor people, of the strikers: "We want to be free." He was assassinated the very next day, April 4, shot on the balcony of the Lorraine Motel.

GARBAGE DOESN'T LIE (IV)

A SHORT HISTORY OF THE GARBAGE CAN

Ghyslain is a garbageman from the sparsely populated region of Brownsburg-Chatham near Montreal. He works his route in shorts and smokes little cigars that give him a distinguished air. He also stands out for his short, nervous strides and keen intelligence. But, like many a garbageman, Ghyslain's a real whiner. It doesn't take much to turn this affable, understanding man into a grumpy toad. "The average person," he's told me more than once, "just needs to be educated. Brought up to speed. They just need to understand. But how can you make someone understand something if you can't even talk to them?"

You may be surprised to learn that there is already a dedicated communication system between garbagemen and the public: the garbage can itself. Ghyslain taught me the language. One day out on the route, I had to bend over backward to retrieve the garbage can from a resident who had jammed it in behind their car. Once emptied, I put it back the right way out. Ghyslain whistled. (That guy has a serious whistle.) The truck stopped on the spot, and so did I.

"Hold up!" he orders. He grabs the garbage can and places it upside down in front of the car. He gives me a look and lets a "huuuuuh" that translates loosely as something like "that should be clear enough for this twit."

It may seem like a small thing, but Ghyslain was teaching me an important lesson. Listen up, good people: Where you find your garbage can after it's emptied has something to tell you. If your garbageman sets it back upside down, don't be offended. That's not negligence, it's common sense: Garbage cans are generally more stable this way, and less likely to fall over. He's just keeping it professional.

But what if you come home to find your garbage can in the middle of your yard? Well, then it's time to ask yourself a few questions. Your garbageman may be sending you a message.

Say I have to dump a bin that has ten gallons of water in it, because you left the lid off, and since you left it out by the roadside for three days the water has had time to make a nice soup with the dog shit tossed in by passersby, and then I had to drag it an extra fifty feet to get around the cars—well, chances are that once I've emptied it out, I'll punch it and then hurl it into the middle of your lawn. If you find your trash can laying in your bed of tulips, assume your garbageman is not a happy camper.

An irate garbageman might go so far as to drag the trash can into the hopper, to smear it with waste and garbage juice. He might actually balance the garbage can *on* the vehicle of an especially hateful resident, and on occasion one might even erect a great wall of trash cans in front of your driveway. This is extreme vexation signaled with ALL CAPS AND TRIPLE EXCLAMATION MARKS!!! On the other hand, in the throes of exasperation, a garbageman might just hurl a can right into the hopper of the truck. And the most virulent expression of displeasure—I've never gone there myself—is to actually dump the garbage onto a vehicle or, under extreme duress, hurl a bag in the direction of the derelict taxpayer.

On the other hand, if you're in the habit of tipping your garbageman—it happens—or if he knows you're elderly or disabled, or if you're just really nice, he'll take the garbage can right back to its place. He might set it upright on the side of the driveway, to make sure it doesn't block the way of other vehicles.

The wealthy enjoy access to this level of service without having to bother to be courteous themselves. In the affluent borough of Westmount, citizens pay for their garbage collectors to pick up their trash cans from a specific spot in their yard and return it to the exact same spot. Valet service, so to speak. And during the holiday season, the upper crust grows amiable. The Christmas spirit loosens the purse strings. Helpers vie for a spot on the Westmount route, where you can rack up the tips, sometimes over a thousand dollars in a day! *Money talks.*

GARBAGEMEN AND SANITATION WORKERS

I meet Raphaël one summer when we're both working for a company called FA. Raphy, as we call him for short, was fresh off the plane from France: mid-forties, Black, and just getting his start in the garbage business in Quebec. At the time, as I mentioned, most garbagemen in Quebec were white—the kind of guys who self-identify as white trash and rednecks. We don't get a lot of yuppies slumming it for a summer or a lot of immigrants, and no students either. Except me, that is. The makeup of his coworkers must have been a real change of scene for Raphy, because in France you find very few white people behind garbage trucks. We were working a route in Montreal North, on Avenue de Cobourg near Boulevard Saint-Michel, running behind a truck driven by a guy named Mimi. A grueling route, as a lot of them are. You might end up running ten miles on a shift, with loads to lift and throw into the hopper every hundred yards or so. Raphaël was dumbstruck. As far as he knew, no route remotely like this existed in France. In the middle of the run, he exclaimed:

"Simon, if we were ever seen running at this pace in France, the newspapers would raise an outcry. Call it modern-day slavery."

Of course, Raphy has the physique for the job. He's slim, tall, and upright, with a frank look in his eyes: a lively, hard-working companion. His movements are measured, with no unnecessary action or wasted energy.

But here in Quebec, his savoir faire brushed up against conceptual roadblocks. Because Raphy is discovering a world he's never known existed. In France, he was a sanitation worker, but that experience taught him little that will transfer over to what we do. He's had to learn the ins and outs of a very different job.

A large portion of French sanitation workers are unionized. Their work is closely supervised, protected, and regulated. Here in Quebec, fifteen years ago, it was the law of the jungle. If you were dragging your ass, a crew might just throw you out on said ass, right on the street corner. Sometimes the truck wouldn't even bother stopping. And if you're just not a good worker? The driver might toss your stuff out the window with a toot of the horn. That way, driver and truck are speaking with one voice, just to make sure you get the message: you're fired!

I once had an interesting conversation with a trainer. He explained to me that when a U.S. firm, Waste Management (WM), was running the market, none of the American managers who'd come visit Quebec could wrap their heads around how much waste our guys could pick up in a day. Compared to the rest of North America, our tonnage was off the charts. We sometimes got over fifty tons per truck per day, and I heard stories of cracking one hundred tons. Meanwhile, most places rarely topped twenty. In France, the average is around six tons, while unionized city workers in Montreal collect around eight tons a day.

Twenty years ago, at WM in the Laurentians, we used to organize competitions for garbage collectors, a bit like the ones you see for lumberjacks or truckers. Race courses were set up and teams vied to finish their sections in the shortest times. The fact that we would celebrate feats of productivity and strength in this way should give you an idea of the spirit of the industry.

Garbageman culture in France is something altogether different. It starts with the name. Garbagemen in France usually go by the title of *éboueur*.[17] What does the word mean, and where does it come from?

Medieval town streets were narrow, winding, shady, poorly ventilated, and rarely paved. There were, in those days, no toilets, and virtually no sewers, so the ground was littered with household refuse, horse dung, pig manure, and human excrement. When it was mixed in with soil and rainwater, this matter turned into a nauseating sludge. As a result, the people who collected it were called mudmen (*boueux* in French), which evolved into the modern-day word *éboueur.*

I don't know how or when the words *vidanges* and *vidangeurs* came to be used in Quebec. And no old dictionary seems to hold the answer. The word *vidange*, which literally means "to empty," was used to refer to emptying cesspools or septic tanks, two objects whose contents are also muddy. It's reasonable to assume that, here in Quebec, the title *vidangeur* was spontaneously attributed to people whose job was to collect solid waste, and that this waste was called *vidanges* by association. At least that's my hypothesis, backed up by the scant sources I have managed to turn up in my research.[18]

In Europe, the collection of waste and sludge has long escaped public regulation. Kings and magistrates did try on occasion to impose their laws on cities, in an attempt to make them more salubrious, with varying degrees of success. The French Revolution may have chopped off the heads of kings and made God tremble—but it was powerless to stem the flow of waste. Waste management has consistently resisted all attempts by public authorities to take charge. It was the preserve of ragpickers, who recovered fabrics, leather, and metal, and independent skilled workers whose trade was the collection and sorting of fecal and organic matter. In the nineteenth century, recycling and repurposing waste played an important role in the economy. Paper was made from the fibers of old rags, and huge sorting centers existed where everything from clothing and furniture to household objects was stored and repurposed; gelatin was rendered from bones—in short, a massive cottage industry repurposed virtually all waste materials, on a permanent basis. But the sensibilities of the wealthy have evolved since the seventeenth century. Bourgeois noses became increasingly intolerant of the pestilential odors emanating from urban garbage. These odors were even suspected of spreading the worst evils.

Then Pasteur's discoveries on germs brought about a sea change in public hygiene. Cleanliness became a national priority. In 1883, Eugène Poubelle, whose role was essentially to administer the city of Paris, passed laws requiring that building owners dispose of their garbage in a purpose-built container named after him, the *poubelle* (still the French term for what we call a trash or garbage can in North America or a dustbin in Britain). Gone the heaps of garbage littering public thoroughfares. A decade later, in Paris, all buildings were connected to the public sewer system, despite the protests of the "mudmen."

France entered the modern era of waste management in the late nineteenth century. Responsibility was transferred to the cities and the State. Perhaps this long history helps explain why garbage collectors are more highly trained in France. To enter the profession there, an aspiring sanitation worker must pass written, physical, and oral exams at a special cleanliness institute, the *École de la Propreté* (Cleanliness School). They also study hazardous materials in special workshops. One private company tried to make courses of this kind a requirement here in Quebec. They are no longer in business.

In France, sanitation workers may sweep streets, pick up cigarette butts, and clean up after demonstrations. The job is a mix of roadwork, public works, and janitorial duties. Some French sanitation workers even do TikToks to raise public awareness of cleanliness issues. Not here. In Quebec, a garbage collector is never a "cleanliness worker." Never!

But what really proved challenging to Raphy wasn't the fact that he'd been to cleanliness school. It was his union culture. As an intelligent and stubborn man, there was no shaking off his very French reflexes—he'd been a union rep himself. Raphy just asked too many questions. He liked bringing up the rules, regulations, and even laws, and subjected our habits to critical scrutiny. For the company, it was unacceptable. And it didn't exactly make other garbagemen eager to work with him.

In Quebec's waste management industry, and in North America more broadly, outside the public sector, people just hate unions. Attempts to unionize are often met with fierce opposition from the employer. And many garbagemen themselves think unions are for whiners, lazy people, and paper pushers.

This anti-union bias is something I know from personal experience. A few years ago, I tried to unionize a garbage collection company. It wasn't so much about better pay as finding a way to make the bosses take our point of view and know-how into account. In this company, white-collar workers enjoyed unheard-of privileges—modern offices, freedom, recognition—while helpers and drivers were subjected to all kinds of stupid control measures. They even started monitoring the drivers with cameras in the cab of the truck! Unbelievable.

So I got in touch with Quebec's largest confederation of labor unions, the CSN, and we held a bunch of meetings. But how can you bring together guys who are geographically dispersed over a vast territory? How do you mobilize a group whose composition is constantly changing? In this business, turnover is high.

At the start of our union drive, our boss painted his colors on the wall.

"If you boys aren't happy, piss off. Think I'll have a hard time finding other employees with no education willing to work for twenty dollars an hour? Go flip burgers for minimum wage!"

The boys had their spirit broken pretty quick. It was a failure, you could say. As for Raphy, he ended up moving on to other opportunities. Probably due to his attitude. He just couldn't let things lie.

ONE BOOK ON WASTE MANAGEMENT that has stayed by my side for years is *Giants of Garbage* by Canadian journalist Harold Crooks.[19] That book is my bible. The central question it asks is a vital one: Is it possible to maintain democratic governance over waste management?

Crooks documents the ways North American cities have been pressured to subcontract garbage collection to private entities. Waste management as we know it has largely developed in opposition to municipal practices. The pattern holds in Greater Montreal as well: municipal expertise, which has traditionally been unionized, has been broken up and replaced first by small contractors and subsequently by big multinationals. Today, the City of Montreal handles less than 5 percent of waste collection on its territory. And it is one of the only municipalities in the region with a municipal collection service.

This laissez-faire capitalist approach to waste management comes with risks. Crooks discusses Walter Lippmann's notion of an "upperworld" and an "underworld," the latter of which arises to protect weak economic actors from unwanted rivals. Networks of underworld players have historically stepped in when legislators removed markets from the legal economy—think prostitution, gambling, drugs today, or alcohol during prohibition. The same has happened in waste management. In some of the worst instances, the underworld has fulfilled "the need for social organization" as the deregulation of waste management has been filled by major conglomerates or organized crime, and frequently some combination of the two.

In Italy's decentralized and fragmented waste management system, the mafia thrives, with all that this implies. "Waste is gold," said one member of the

Camorra (the Neapolitan mafia), referring to the traffic in toxic waste, whose revenues in Italy are estimated at fourteen billion euros.

Of course, entrusting waste management to gangsters and racketeers has repercussions. In Naples, the mafia has buried toxic waste everywhere, creating crisis after scandal for years. In an area known as the "triangle of death," cancer rates have soared, fields are poisoned, the rivers stink. It's a plague.[20]

Waste management by vast private monopolies is a more respectable enterprise. Or at least, that's how it looks, if we confine our perspective to North America. But when we widen our view to explore the global industry, the picture grows cloudier. Massive corporations are adept at finding loopholes and slipping between the cracks of laws and regulations, and are experts in the art of applying pressure to create a legislative environment favorable to their interests.

It is perhaps not a stretch to say that there is no such thing as real democratic control of large-scale capitalist enterprise. Working for these conglomerates gives you a taste of the same control and endless bureaucracy as when you try to deal with civil servants, without any of the rights that come with being a resident of a city or citizen of a country.

Those of us on the front lines have a different, first-hand experience of what it feels like when big industry players implement complex and fastidious policies and practices. Mostly, all this approach does is add a layer of annoyance.

When the French waste management conglomerate Derichebourg began doing business in Quebec, it tried to impose its European corporate culture on North America. The company had a fleet of brand-new hybrid trucks—beautiful, state-of-the-art machines that had the drawback of being incredibly slow. That about summed it up. The venture didn't even last two years. Derichebourg ended up having to subcontract many of its routes to smaller brokers. And when it did, productivity doubled. As a rule, this hybrid system of conglomerates subcontracting to brokers is what you find in Greater Montreal.

And I have to admit that this system suits me fine. As it happens, I hate the very idea of a Cleanliness

School and the overregulated life of civil servants in equal measure, neither more nor less than I abhor the violence of the underworld and the organizational culture of international conglomerates. It just doesn't work for me. From where I stand, none of these management systems listens to the garbagemen themselves; none of them trusts our experience, considers making us part of the actual waste management processes, or cares about our culture. None of them, even those under municipal or government jurisdiction, are in any real way democratic, as I understand the term. But then, who'd consider asking a garbageman for advice on democracy?

I have the soul of a ragpicker, those proudly free and fiercely independent waste collectors who in Paris fiercely opposed the new laws of Eugène Poubelle and the other architects of modern public sanitation. I recognize myself in the anger of the Parisian mudmen who stood against the policy of the *tout-à-l'égout* system of dumping everything in the new sewers, which meant routing latrine sludge—a material previously harvested and sold as fertilizer to farmers—into the sea. Politically, I guess you could call me an anarcho-garbageman. I dream of a world where the castoffs of society self-manage the project of managing its waste.

As a mercenary, I make my living by slipping through the cracks of the system, working with the brokers who do the bidding of massive conglomerates. Some of these brokers feel a little like a mafia, others are more aboveboard, but all are ingeniously adept at walking fine lines and bending rules where they have to. By operating in between the many links in the chain, I dream of the freedom and fraternity of the Parisian ragpickers. I should have shared this ideal with Raphy. Equality, freedom, fraternity: those are notions Raphy would have understood.

A PASSION FOR GARBAGE

Not long ago I watched a television show about garbagemen in Quebec, *Les Éboueurs*. It's typical reality TV: we ride along with garbagemen working in all kinds of conditions. On the one hand, I was proud to see my fellow garbagemen on TV. But the show also left me ambivalent. It was the same feeling I had watching a news segment where a young journalist worked as a garbage collector for a week, and his team captured it on video.[21] Both shows depict garbagemen in a sympathetic light. And both were critical of the pace of work and the pressure the system puts on us, and how that can translate into safety concerns. Both shows are well-intentioned; both present observations that are for the most part accurate—and yet . . .

When I ask my buddy Steve about the shows, he told me there was something that stuck in his craw about the overall sense it conveys of our daily lives. For the average person watching the show, the takeaway is something like this: working in garbage collection is a shitty job, poor unfortunate people who have to do it, they're exploited by a cruel system, so let's treat them with compassion. Now, Steve is proud as a peacock, and he just *loves* being a garbageman. So the idea of showing viewers that we're deserving of their *compassion* came as a slap to the face.

I think Steve's exaggerating a bit when he says the two shows reduce us to caricatures. Both paint a fairly balanced picture, in their own way. But what the journalists and production teams failed to capture is the ineffable reason Steve and I and so many other garbagemen love what we do. Even with the best of intentions, they can't fathom why anyone in their right mind could possibly *want* to be a garbageman. Trust me, it's perfectly possible to do this job because you want to. Many of us do.

If you told me I was going to die tomorrow, I'd go out for one final run on the back of a truck, without a second thought. I'd go right back where I belong. Running behind a garbage truck brings me profound satisfaction and great joy. It's an activity that can satisfy my desire to push myself physically and be the best version of myself. I guess I'm a jock at heart. I need to be out moving, doing physical exercise, pushing myself to new extremes. A friend of mine who's a serious sports fan and follows pro leagues once told me that I was the best nonprofessional athlete he knew. And he's not wrong to draw this parallel.

The *Éboueurs* reality show even challenged André Roy, a former National Hockey League player, to try his hand at garbage collection for four hours, which is of course not even a full shift! On the ice, Roy had been a rough-and-tumble left-winger, the kind of guy known for grinding in the corners. An energy player.

A sturdy dude, six foot four, over two hundred pounds. A big, tough guy, for sure—yet when they put him behind a truck, he couldn't hack it for more than *one hour*. They burned him out, and he threw in the towel.

I've always thought that what makes a good helper is the ability to sublimate your impulses and transform them into productive gestures. For many people who have had challenging life experiences, their impulses are negative forces. Becoming a garbageman demands exceptional mastery of physical strength and willpower. It's not dissimilar to the discipline that top athletes develop over their bodies and minds. But when athletes do it, they have their eyes on a different prize: win medals, break records, entertain the masses with their exploits. And they have the support of a massive system: the media, political forces, and society at large are united in glorifying their performances. Athletes are applauded, admired, and earn small or large fortunes.

When I finish a shift, I've run fifteen miles. I've put my back under duress and taken considerable personal risks to keep your neighborhood clean and healthy. And pretty much no one cares.

It's considered normal for an athlete to get injured. And when they do, they receive the best possible care. For humble wage slaves like us, it's another story. We're accused of negligence, denied paid leave. Public colleges in Quebec have physiotherapists on hand to treat swimmers in swim clubs, but we garbagemen are generally left to grin and bear it.

Whenever my mother talks about my job, she never fails to remind me of all the times I've gotten injured. The implication is clear: I should just ditch this dangerous job. If I were a professional hockey player getting showered with money and glory, with an elite medical team to look after me, I doubt she'd constantly harp on my injuries and the risks of my job. Yet it's these very things—risk and physical intensity—that make the garbageman's job so exceptional. In my opinion, a garbageman's performance is on par with that of an Olympic marathon runner or a pro hockey defenseman. But no one would ever think of comparing the two activities. In our society, sports is a highly lucrative spectacle. We couldn't say the same about garbage disposal. Above all, elite sports reflects the values and ideals of the upper classes: be a winner, dominate others, and enjoy the means to lead a life of leisure.

Our work as garbagemen resembles elite sports for its combination of performance, toil, and pushing yourself to new feats. But our extreme sport is performed for members of the lower classes. In our world, that's enough to belittle you. The garbageman puts his health at risk for society as a whole. He takes great pride in it. But workers' strength is a commodity to be exploited until their dying day, with no regard for their well-being or will. And if we do care about workers' safety, that care takes the form of drawing up regulations and tying them up in bureaucratic red tape, a surefire way to kill the joy in any job.

THE JOY OF THROWING TRASH finds its expression in the beauty and simplicity of our art form. Experienced guys will recognize the signature of a helper glimpsed behind a truck in the distance: the way he picks up bags, heaves a trash can high, or runs from pile to pile; the distinct pitch of his intensity. That guy carrying three trash cans in one hand and a hot-water tank in the other could only be Gratton, making his way over to the truck and launching the contents of each can into the hopper with astonishing assurance. And there's Steve, indefatigable as ever, stopping cars with no more than a hand signal and natural authority as he powers through his run. And there's big Oli, the dude who never takes a break, gathering the cans and bags together while the truck goes off to empty at the dump. As for me, I'm the guy who's still out at 10:00, running at the same pace I set at 7:00 a.m. As if I were just getting started.

We can't forget the drivers, who have to exercise tight control over massive machines that don't like being tamed. The helper has to adjust their pace to the truck, so we don't slow down the operation; the driver has to temper his truck's impatience, its tendency to speed up, by working in tacit agreement with his helper. The way this waltz plays out is that the machine and the workload impose a pace on the garbagemen, forcing them to push themselves to new heights of endurance, at risk of losing control of the situation. This performance yields an undefinable sense of vitality and accomplishment. It's a dizzying, exhausting movement, an intoxicating pressure, a state of grace that frees you for a while from the burdens of existence. We fear it, and we seek it out—over and over, in an endless cycle.

I know how to do a lot of different things. I've been a frontline outreach worker, done some freelance journalism, and conducted research, but I always come back to the garbage—or, strictly speaking, I never left. It would not be an exaggeration to say that my passion for waste collection approaches a calling. People are constantly amazed. "Aren't you tired of running? You know you could do something different." (Read: better.) It's not easy to understand the passion that garbagemen like me carry inside.

"Do you love it?" is one of the first things I ask new employees. Because if you don't, this job is impossible. Instead of harnessing the machine and directing the waltz of waste, you'll get crushed by it. It'll take your health, if not your life. That's the price you pay to be an elite athlete in the sport of garbage collection.

FREEGANISM

Spend enough time with garbage and you may learn to love it—I know I have. It may sound strange to most, and even twisted to some, but if you pass me on the street on my day off, there's a good chance I'll have a piece of salvaged junk in my hands. I'm a gleaner, a picker, a collector—the names vary, but the act stays the same. When there's something I need, I'll often put off buying it, convinced that with a little patience I'll find exactly what I'm looking for on the side of the road. It's second nature to me.

When I was in university, I drove to class not because it was too far but so I could pick things up along the way. Furniture, toys, items to sell, nonferrous metals for the scrapyard, whatever. And when I go out for an evening walk, you'll see me opening up the bins in my neighborhood, panning for gold. Often, I'm thinking of someone I know who mentioned something they need. My father-in-law wants a new cooler? Two weeks later, I'll show up with three. Because I want to give him a choice, and also because I want him to be able to make up his mind quickly, so I don't end up with a dozen coolers cluttering up my house.

At any moment I'm liable to hitch up my trailer and go for a solo mission in search of "oversized objects." Within a few hours, I can pick up pretty much everything you'd need to furnish an apartment. That's exactly what I did, for my first home.

Freeganism is the term for this lifestyle. It's based on a fundamental rejection of the premises of consumer society. Freeganism is a philosophical, ethical, economic, and political stance, and after twenty years of filling garbage dumps, it's the only one that makes sense to me.

I've grown highly organized in my recycling sideline. I've got a person who sells secondhand items for me. I go to flea markets several times a year to sell off my surplus. And I give large amounts to donation centers. I've recycled prodigious quantities of precious and strategic nonferrous metals, like copper. This work of mine reduces the ecological footprint of my household and vehicles, while also providing a nontrivial extra income stream. Last but not least, I'm diverting metals from landfills, metals that are destined to become increasingly scarce, or even disappear, given the huge demand for them as a result of the energy transition the politicians are preparing for us.

Being a freegan also means maintaining a healthy respect for the materials, products, and the entire production chain. I'm against the atrocious working conditions of the people in Bangladesh and other countries who make most of our clothing. I don't want to encourage this exploitation. I think I've bought fewer than five pieces of clothing in the last twenty years.

There's nothing revolutionary about being a freegan. It's a way of life and an economic practice that has the merit of truly limiting the orgy of commodities that is our capitalist society. The plain truth is that we already have enough stuff. There's no need to make more. Fixing a shovel by replacing its handle just makes more sense to me than buying a new one. Today's scrap dealers and freegans are perpetuating the age-old way of life of the ragpickers of yesteryear. We can be found in every corner of the planet. In China today, people recycle and salvage in every corner of the country, without being ordered to do so by any company or state. Wherever you go, you will find people who understand that waste is wrong, and marvel at the many discoveries they make in the trash. One person's trash is another's treasure. We are the resistance, fighting against the excesses of the waste management system.

Freeganism as a way of life still needs to be better organized, here in Quebec. We exist on the margins of the margins. We've got networks of *ressourceries*, and even some free stores, but nothing like ReTuna, a shopping mall near Stockholm, Sweden, dedicated entirely to recycling, recovery, and the sharing economy.[22] Something must be done to make this alternative waste management system more attractive and economically viable.

For example, I've never understood why scrap dealers and other gleaners don't get back part of the taxes cities collect for waste management. By diverting materials from landfills, they are saving citizens' costs that could finance their activity.

In cities, where there's no shortage of fodder for black humor, we speak of "waste recovery" when industries do things like capture methane gas from landfill sites and convert it into gas. Yet we act as if scrappers aren't recovering anything. My overall sense is that we live in a system bent on perpetuating production for production's sake, waste, and the destruction of the world. I'm a cog in the wheels of the system. But I'm also, in my modest way, a grain of sand slowing the works, rebelling against a system whose premises I reject.

GARBAGE DOESN'T LIE (V)

THE GUTTED BAG

A gutted bag lies on the ground in a sunken heap, abandoned in an alley in Montreal's Milton Parc district. Maybe the harsh winter conditions have taken their toll. Or maybe someone grinding out a living in the area tore the bag open in the hopes of salvaging something valuable: a returnable bottle, a piece of clothing, something to eat. Maybe this unfortunate bag got run over by a car. One thing is certain: the chaos of life in the street has had its way with this bag, which has taken its revenge by spilling its guts out all over the sidewalk.

Every spring is the same story. The thaw comes, the snow melts after long months of winter, and Montrealers lament their city's filthiness. Abandoned garbage dumps, overfilled garbage cans, discarded papers, bottles, and dishes resurface. It's the garbage zombie apocalypse: last year's trash springs back from the dead! A veritable garbage invasion. Journalists get up in arms. What are we waiting for to clean up this mess? What a disgrace. The gutted bag greets these grand declarations with a smile. "Oh, look at the pigs! Suddenly surprised to wake up and see that they live in a sty!"

The attitude of the "average person" never ceases to amaze me. They might come over to the truck while we're working, come right up to us, and toss a bag of trash at our feet—sometimes literally right at us!—without having the common decency to look at us, let alone thank us. These people thank the courier for delivering their packages, the mover, and the mail carrier. They have no problem chatting with road workers.

But they barely see the garbageman. They wish we could be invisible, just as they hope their garbage will magically disappear. But then the annual thaw comes around and the city looks suddenly gray, dusty, and strewn with garbage, and now here they suddenly are, shouting it from the rooftops—"What are the garbagemen doing about this?"

Not a hard question! We're out on the streets, working up a sweat running a goddamn marathon trying to keep our cities clean. Because our entire society is an insurmountable pile of filth, like the Augean stables in the Fifth Labor of Heracles. And yes, we are Heracles in this analogy.

One day, a kindhearted garbage collector will bend down and pick up the gutted bag. He'll pick it up gently and toss it into the hopper of his truck, where it can finally rest in peace.

And the grateful bag will recite this secular prayer, borrowed from the poet Jacques Prévert. *Je vous salue ma rue pleine de grâce, l'éboueur est avec nous.*

I salute you, street full of grace, the garbageman is here for us.

AUTHOR'S ACKNOWLEDGMENTS

First, I'd like to thank the instigator of this project, Alain Deneault. I was fortunate to cross paths with someone whose sincere interest gave me the impetus to get started.

My gratitude also to my publisher and editor at Lux, Mark Fortier, without whom this story would have never made it onto paper. Mark had the vision to summon the discourse inside and help fashion it into a coherent narrative. Though I was a stranger in the world of books and publishing, Alain and Mark believed in me and my project, and I thank them for their confidence.

Working with my French-languages publisher, Lux, was my introduction to the publishing world. I now understand that a book is not the work of its author alone: it is absolutely a team effort. Thank you, Lux!

Thanks also to Pablo Strauss for this translation, which in places is almost an adaptation that manages to do justice to the original while giving it a new life. Thanks, Pablo!

I would also like to express my gratitude to Melville House Publishing, for believing in this book's value for readers in the United States and beyond, and for approaching it with such respect and care.

Thanks also to my family. I know that the many times I had to step away to write were times when my wife, Laurianne, had to make up for my absence at home. A book is a team, and it's also a web of relationships that the author is one part of. That makes me think of Daniel, my father, who I lost during the writing process. Unbeknownst to him, he indirectly contributed to the existence of this book on the "world of garbage."

And last but definitely not least, my heartfelt thanks to my coworkers, most of whom have no idea I've written a book about our world. I also have no idea whether they'll hear about it one day, or if it will interest them. When I write a story, as a journalist, I make it clear to participants that the result depends on their testimony and that, ultimately, reporting is a form of collaboration. I like to think of my coworkers as collaborators who made it possible to produce the book we now hold in our hands. Thanks, guys!

TRANSLATOR'S ACKNOWLEDGMENTS

First, I would like to thank the author for his gracious help and fascinating conversation. I am grateful to this book's editor, Dennis Johnson, and its managing editor, Mike Lindgren, for steering the text toward a place of greater clarity. Anonymous strangers on the r/garbagemen subreddit provided invaluable help with terminology. David Hagen, who has taught me so much as a translator, gave me sensible suggestions. And last but not least, thanks to all the garbagemen and other sanitation workers keeping the streets of all our cities clean and clear!

ENDNOTES

1 The *roman du terroir* (novel of the land) was a prominent literary genre in Quebec from the mid-nineteenth to the mid-twentieth century. Typical novels celebrate the honorable working people and traditional values of Quebec's rural society.

2 Plume Latraverse, "Moé, j'aime pas ça travailler" (1978).

3 There are many words for this position, depending on the region, including *helper*, *thrower*, and *loader*.

4 Z. Bauman, *Wasted Lives: Modernity and Its Outcasts* (Polity: 2017).

5 Pope Francis, "Apostolic Exhortation Evangelii Gaudium of the Holy Father Francis to the Bishops, Clergy, Consecrated Persons and the Lay Faithful on the Proclamation of the Gospel in Today's World (Vatican Press, 2013).

6 Figures from the United Nations Environment Programme (UNEP), *Global Waste Management Outlook 2024*.

7 B. London, "Ending the Depression through Planned Obsolescence" (self-published, 1932). Full text available on Wikimedia Commons. This discussion of London's life and thought here draws heavily on Giles Slade's *Made to Break: Technology and Obsolescence in America* (Harvard UP, 2016).

8 See Kristin Houser, "Why Is a Strange Plastic Crust Spreading on This Island's Coast?" *Futurism* (blog), June 24, 2019; I. Gestoso, E. Cacabelos, P. Ramalhosa, and J. Canning-Clode, "Plasticrusts: A New Potential Threat in the Anthropocene's Rocky Shores," *Science of the Total Environment* 687 (2019): 413–415.

9 See, for example: Laura Sullivan, "How Big Oil Misled the Public into Believing Plastic Would Be Recycled," *NPR*, September 11, 2022; Center for Climate Integrity, "Not Just Climate: Big Oil Lied About Plastic Recycling, Too, and Must Be Held Accountable," February 15, 2024.

10 Peter Zimonjic, "Poilievre Promises to Scrap Single-Use Plastics Ban and Bring Back the Plastic Straw," *CBC News*, April 18, 2025.

11 G. Shochat and C. Lavigne, "How Canadian Recycling Could Be Fuelling Pollution in India," *CBC News*, February 10, 2022.

12 Sophia Samantaroy, "Nearly 30 Metric Tonnes of Plastic Are Improperly Burned Every Year—with Broad, Unexplored Health Impacts," *Health Policy Watch*, September 16, 2024.

13 M. Le Meur, *Le mythe du recyclage* (Premier Parallèle, 2021).

14 A Fourrier, "Le poids du désordre," *Liberté* 338 (2023).

15 R. Oldenziel and H. Weber, "Introduction: Reconsidering Recycling," *Contemporary European History* 22, no. 3 (2013): 347–370.

16 The fascinating story behind this Quebec popular anthem can be read in the online *Canadian Encyclopedia* article "Mon Pays."

17 Variations include *ripeur* and *agent de propreté*.

18 C. Richard, "Cachez ce déchet que je ne saurais voir: la mise en place d'un service municipal de collecte et d'élimination des matières résiduelles à Montréal (1868–1920)," (master's thesis). Université du Québec à Montréal (2022).

19 H. Crooks, *Giants of Garbage: The Rise of the Global Waste Industry and the Politics of Pollution Control* (James Lorimer & Company, 1993).

20 A. Giuffrida, "'Triangle of Death': Will Italy Finally Tackle Mafia's Toxic Waste Dumping?," *The Guardian*, February 18, 2025.

21 Jean Balthazard, Daphnée Hacker-B, and Matt Joycey, "Dans la peau d'un éboueur," *tabloid.co* (blog).

22 *Ressourceries* in Quebec are generally large thrift stores with a social mission.

Photos of the author at work by Laurianne Desjardins

Photos on pp. 138 & 154: Réal Saint-Jean, *Grèves des cols bleus (1972)*, BAnQ, Archives nationales à Montréal, fonds *La Press*, 06MP833

ABOUT THE AUTHOR

SIMON PARÉ-POUPART became a garbageman in Montréal to pay for his college education. He has now been a garbageman for twenty years, while earning graduate degrees in sociology and international business and working as a journalist and social worker. He lives in Montreal, Québec.

ABOUT THE TRANSLATOR

PABLO STRAUSS has translated numerous books from Québec French into English and is a three-time finalist for the Governor General's Literary Award for translation. His translation of Éric Chacour's *Ce que je sais de toi* was a shortlisted finalist for two Writers' Trust of Canada awards. He lives in Québec City.